# Living with Cancer

# LIVING WITH CANCER

## Dr Rosy Daniel

Robinson
London

Constable and Robinson Ltd
3 The Lanchesters,
162 Fulham Palace Road,
London W6 9ER

First published by Robinson, an imprint of
Constable & Robinson Ltd, 2000

A copy of the British Library Cataloguing in Publication Data for
this title is available from the British Library

ISBN 1 84119 163 9

Edited and designed by
EMS Editorial Services, Shalbourne,
Marlborough, Wiltshire SN8 3QJ

**Important Note**
This book is not intended to be a substitute for medical advice or
treatment. Any person with a condition requiring medical attention
should consult a qualified medical practitioner or suitable therapist.

Printed and bound in the EC

# Dedication

This book is dedicated to my dearest friends, Penny Brohn, and her supporter and co-founder of the Bristol Cancer Help Centre, Pat Pilkington.

Words cannot express my love and admiration for Pat and Penny, and for the sheer determination, bravery, wit and creative intelligence they brought to bear in founding the Bristol Approach to cancer. I am deeply enriched by the experience of having known and worked with them both, and for the special privilege of helping to care for Penny. I am honoured to pass on their teachings and insights in this book, and I congratulate the Centre wholeheartedly for its profound contribution to medicine and to the care of people with cancer in this its twentieth year of existence.

# Contents

# Foreword

Occasionally, Western medicine seems unsure of its own identity. The public is endlessly bombarded with propaganda heralding new, more powerful, more scientific, more hi-tech, more expensive treatment, today's latest scientific achievement or tomorrow's breakthrough. And why not? The improvements have been dazzling. The X-ray was developed only just over a century ago. Advances in medical technology followed in an unceasing stream, including the electrocardiogram to monitor heart conditions and, from the 1920s, electron microscopes, permitting investigation of cell pathology. More recent years have brought endoscopes, lasers, ultrasound and scanners. And practical consequences have followed. One milestone was the first surgical intervention, just over 50 years ago, for 'blue babies' born with congenital heart disease. Open heart surgery dates from the 1950s; by-pass operations began in 1967. Surgery became like space travel, boldly going where none had gone before. Organ replacement was developed, first with kidneys, and heart transplants became banner headlines in 1967.

For the future, the Human Genome Project – the offspring of new theories and new scientific disciplines like molecular biology – affords us still further prospects of new breakthroughs. We already have a sound grasp of the genetic basis of terrible disorders like muscular dystrophy, Tay-Sachs disease, Huntington's disease, and cystic fibrosis. There is every likelihood that other crippling and fatal conditions will turn out to be genetically programmed, perhaps even some cancers. As in every other department of medicine, understanding is sure to lead to therapeutic action. Medicine has relieved mankind of many scourges; helped by the Genome Project, the twenty-first century seems set fair to be the age when the burden of genetic disorders is finally lifted.

But doctors, scientists, and their publicists sometimes seem to forget that there is more to medicine than that. Medicine is an art as well as a science, and the healing art is holistic through and through. It must touch all aspects of the sick person – the mind as well as the body, the soul, spirit or feelings as well as the reason, and the unconscious as well as the conscious. And it must be interactive, a dialogue between the sick person and the healer. The word 'patient' comes from the Latin for passive, but it is vital that the patient should be an agent as well.

The holistic approach to health is widely associated with various sorts of 'alternative medicine', Western and Eastern alike. And rightly so. But they are also integral to the mainstream history of conventional medicine, and have been so ever since the Greeks immortally inscribed in the Hippocratic Oath the promise 'above all, to do no harm'.

The medicine of antiquity, which was transmitted to Islam and then back to the medieval West, and which remained powerful throughout the Renaissance, paid great attention to general health maintenance through regulation of diet, exercise, hygiene and lifestyle. In the absence of decisive anatomical and physiological expertise, and without the benefit of a powerful arsenal of cures and surgical skills, the ability to diagnose and make prognoses was highly valued, and an intimate physician–patient relationship was fostered. The teachings of antiquity – which remained authoritative into the eighteenth century and still supply reservoirs of medical folklore – were more successful in helping people to cope with chronic conditions, and in soothing lesser ailments, than in conquering the life-threatening infections that became endemic and epidemic in the civilized world – leprosy, plague, smallpox, measles, and, later, the 'filth diseases' (like typhus) associated with urban squalor.

This rather personal tradition of bedside medicine long remained popular in the West, as did its equivalents in Chinese and Ayurvedic medicine. But in Europe it was supplemented and challenged by the creation of a more 'scientific' type of medicine, grounded, for the first time, upon experimental anatomical and physiological investigation, epitomized, from the fifteenth century, by the dissection techniques that were to become central to medical education. Landmarks in this programme include the publication of *On the Fabric of the Human Body* (1543) by the Paduan professor, Andreas Vesalius, the first momentous anatomical atlas and a work that challenged truths received since Galen; and William Harvey's *On the Motion of the Heart* (1628), which put physiological enquiry on the map through experiments demonstrating the circulation of the blood and the role of the heart as a pump. Thereafter 'scientic medicine' took off.

But its achievements must not blind us to the fact that both sides of medicine – the humane and personal no less than the scientific – are equally important and central to our medical tradition. As this absorbing book shows, the Bristol Cancer Help Centre is dedicated to upholding and integrating both. In one light it may be viewed as pioneering 'alternative approaches', but these are, in their own way, central to what medicine has always been about.

*Roy Porter*
*Wellcome Institute for the History of Medicine, London*

# *Preface*

The main reason for writing this book is to help people with cancer to understand the pivotal role they can play in their own healing and recovery process. In the minds of many people, cancer is a one-way street, and the diagnosis of cancer equates to a death sentence. This is very wrong. There are huge numbers of people who recover from cancer and many documented cases of 'spontaneous remission' or 'remarkable recovery' from supposedly 'terminal' cancer. There is great variation in the periods of remission or disease-free interval in people who apparently have the same sorts of cancer, and so it is clear that there are many factors other than medical treatments that determine whether one lives with, or dies from, cancer.

During the 20 years of work and study at the Bristol Cancer Help Centre, it has been possible to identify many of the factors that can change the odds for someone diagnosed with cancer, and it is clear that many of these factors are ones over which the individual can take control. Of these, probably the most important of all is taking control itself. Most obviously, this means becoming actively involved in your own care and management, i.e., taking yourself out of the passenger seat – the passive, dependent, patient role – and placing yourself firmly in the driving seat. The other factors are mediated through specific healthcare interventions, which all help to promote optimum health in the presence of illness, however severe the illness may be.

It is hoped that in explaining how this active role can be assumed, this book will help people to find the hope, inspiration, support and guidance that will enable them to cope with the frightening challenge of their illness. More than this, it is hoped that through taking this approach your experience of cancer may be transformed – as it has been for many – from a crisis into an opportunity, a chance to embark upon a far happier, healthier, and more fulfilling lifestyle than you had before diagnosis.

The second aim is to address the vulnerability of those caring for people with cancer: to look at the stress and distress associated with their role and legitimize their need for support and help, too. Supporters will be encouraged to protect themselves from the risks associated with the high demands and trauma of living with life-threatening illness in a loved one, to learn how to protect and care for themselves, and in so doing maximize their ability to offer support and help to the one they are caring for.

The third aim is to clarify for healthcare professionals (HCPs) involved in the care of people with cancer the importance of both complementary therapies and self-help approaches in the hospital and hospice settings for supportive care; further, it aims to highlight the difference between this and the very active and personally empowering holistic health model used by people who embark upon the Bristol Cancer Help Centre's programme.

It is hoped that HCPs will be able to understand the value of the Bristol Approach, both to people with cancer and to those who support them, so that they will not only tolerate but actively encourage those who wish to use the holistic approach. In describing what happens when people move into a dynamic, healthy relationship with themselves, and become actively involved in their own care, it is hoped that the value – indeed, the need – for this approach will become abundantly clear. Even better, it might tempt them to train in and seek holistic help for themselves because this will be the real way that healthy evolution towards the integrated medicine of the future will be assured.

# Introduction

The British Cancer Help Centre, a small independent charity established in 1980, has from the very beginning existed exclusively to help people with cancer and their supporters using the holistic approach to healthcare. Each year, up to 1,000 people attend the Centre on a residential basis to take part in our therapy courses; many more use our helpline, community and information services, and the Centre also has an important role in the education of health professionals.

The Centre was the first holistic cancer care unit in the UK, and the long experience we have gained in working with people with cancer means that we are regarded as providing the 'gold standard' in complementary cancer care. Nowadays, people come from all over the world to receive help or to learn about using the Bristol Approach.

Although the Centre works hard to extend its services each year, the number of people requiring help also rises, and the Centre cannot hope to embrace everyone personally who needs its support. This book has therefore been written to allow many more people with cancer to understand our approach and to use some of the helpful techniques we have developed in the Centre over the past 20 years.

At whatever stage people find themselves on their own personal cancer journeys we know from experience that our complementary and self-help healing programme can both generate a real sense of hope and provide practical assistance, and that the person in charge of this process is you. The holistic approach draws on centuries of healing techniques and understanding from both European and Eastern traditions, and works very well when it is integrated with conventional treatment, including chemotherapy, radiotherapy and surgery.

We hope that this book will be of direct use to you, for whatever reason you are reading it, and we send you from the Centre every good wish for your future health and healing.

*Christopher Head, Chief Executive,*
*Bristol Cancer Help Centre*

# PART ONE

# SETTING THE FRAMEWORK

# 1

# *The Bristol Approach*

## Greetings from Bristol

Penny Brohn – co-founder of the Bristol Cancer Help Centre – lived with breast cancer for 20 years. In the pages that follow, you will read about many others who have either made remarkable recoveries or are managing to live in equilibrium with their cancer. You will learn about the holistic approach to health and illness, the science underpinning it, and the different therapies and self-help techniques that you can use to strengthen your health, increase your tolerance of conventional treatments, and enhance your chances of recovery.

It is hoped that this book will help you to recognize the crucial role that you can play in your recovery process, and, most important of all, that your sense of hope and control will begin to return. Many thousands of people with cancer have used the Bristol Approach to turn the crisis of cancer into an opportunity, and we sincerely hope that this will become possible for you, too.

The importance of coming to Bristol was the fact that I turned around my whole thought process. I came feeling frightened. I had been told that I had three months to live. The orthodox medicine could do nothing for me and I was just delighted that I could take charge of my own life. I was taught that there were various practices

3

that I could follow – meditation, visualization and relaxation, and a host of other things, and these I followed. It was quite hard in the first place to get into it but I'm sure they made all the difference to my recovery.

*Laura Newcombe: living with inoperable*
*bladder cancer, diagnosed in 1985*

# An Inspired Idea

The Bristol Cancer Help Centre was the brainchild of acupuncturist Penny Brohn and her close friend Pat Pilkington. Penny was diagnosed with breast cancer in 1979 whilst she was in her early thirties and with three small children under ten years old. Driven by the imperative to stay alive for them, combined with an acute sense of the inadequacy of the medical model in dealing with both her and her cancer, she set about discovering alternative ways to beat her disease. Strongly encouraged by Pat, she embarked on her healing journey, which was to take her all over the world, inspire the creation of the Bristol Cancer Help Centre, launch her into a media career, and enable her to live with cancer for 20 years from the point of her diagnosis.

Her search for alternative medicines that would combat the cancer by strengthening her body's immune system took her first to the metabolic clinic of Dr Josef Issels in Bavaria for immunotherapy. Later she went to the clinic of Dr Ernesto Contreras in Mexico to have metabolic therapy. Back in England she attended the Mind Body Centre of Isobel and Maxwell Cade in London, had acupuncture with her long-time mentor Dr Tony Evans, and had spiritual healing with the Reverend Tim Tiley in Bristol. She also visited a remote monastery in the Welsh mountains for meditation retreats.

It was during the nine weeks in Issels' clinic, whilst undergoing a particularly rigorous treatment, that Penny broke down to Pat, telling her that whilst she knew this alternative medicine for her body was right, it was really her soul and emotions that were in complete turmoil and desperately needing help. She was terrified of dying, devastated at the thought of leaving her children motherless, and still full of grief having recently lost both parents within weeks of each other. She was also struggling with marital conflicts that had undermined her considerably and left her feeling very isolated.

This sense of isolation was now multiplied a thousand fold as she lay in a German clinic, miles from her family and friends, shivering with fever induced by Dr Issels to boost her immune system. The bottom had completely dropped out of her world. Her heartfelt wish, which she expressed there and then to Pat, was for a place where all of these treatments and therapies could be brought together under one roof; where body, mind and spirit could be thought about simultaneously – a place under strong medical guidance where all this fear could be contained and all levels of being could be cared for and involved in the process of self-healing.

Pat picked up Penny's thread immediately, asking her how such a centre would be, what it would look like, and what staff and therapies there would be. Fifteen minutes earlier, Penny had been a completely devastated wreck; now, as she built in her mind the ideal centre for people with cancer, she was transformed – absolutely buzzing – as she poured out idea after idea. After about half an hour of this torrent of creativity she suddenly stopped, realized what was happening, and with total conviction said to Pat, 'This is us, Pat, this is what we have got to do. We have to build the Cancer Help Centre.'

As utterly daunting as this felt, with Penny sick and both of them identifying themselves more as housewife than as entrepreneur, they knew immediately that this was it – they would indeed go on to work together to manifest the vision they had created that day. They spent the rest of that week designing and refining their concept. They already had a building, in Downfield Road, Bristol, which Pat and her husband, Canon Christopher Pilkington, had bought to use as a spiritual healing centre. Christopher had latterly spent much of his time developing his ability as a healer under the tutelage of Reverend Tim Tiley, and Pat and Penny knew that he would be only too happy to add his support and services to their project. They had friends who were nutritional therapists, so they knew it would be easy to provide expert dietary advice as part of their programme. Counsellors, too, they knew would be no problem to find. The major sticking point was the question of where they would find a doctor in England wanting to work in an holistic way with the treatment of cancer. As Penny said to Pat, 'Why would I be over here in Bavaria miles from my children if there was one single holistic doctor in Britain who was thinking along these lines.'

## The First Centre

They came home with this question raging in their minds, only to find that whilst they were in Bavaria Christopher had received a letter from Dr Alec Forbes, a retiring consultant physician who was 'looking for somewhere to put into practice his ideas about the holistic treatment of cancer'. If they had needed any more confirmation that this idea had their name on it this was it. Very soon Alec was appointed the first Medical Director of the newly named 'Bristol Cancer Help Centre', and they opened on an entirely voluntary basis one day a week at the house in Downfield Road.

Very quickly the news got around and they were soon full to overflowing with people who were immensely grateful for the support and guidance. Word rapidly reached the BBC about 'this strange place in Clifton giving everybody pints of carrot juice and mountains of rabbit food', and two programmes were made: one by a Scottish company for their series 'The Visit', and one by a BBC journalist who was dispatched to do an exposé about this 'cancer quackery'. However, the journalist who came from the BBC was so moved by what he experienced that he subsequently made a six-part documentary for

BBC2's '40 Minutes' series, following the progress of six individuals through their healing process over several months.

This series, which was shown in Britain in early 1983, caused an avalanche. The note that had been struck by Penny, Pat, Christopher and Alec resonated deeply with many thousands of people with cancer world wide, and within weeks the system at Bristol was in complete log-jam as demand far exceeded what they could provide. It also became apparent that a day visit to the Centre was not sufficient to enable individuals to cover the ground necessary in order to make the deeper healing changes that are needed to strengthen their chances of recovery. It was now evident that residential premises were required.

Suddenly they were in the big league and were negotiating for large residential premises in the heart of Georgian Clifton. The move to Grove House took place in 1983, and the new centre was opened on 15 July, by His Royal Highness The Prince of Wales, who expressed his wholehearted support for the holistic mind, body, spirit approach to healing that was being promoted by Bristol. With this move came the need to go from being a voluntary organization to being a fundraising charity employing staff to run the expanding therapy programme. However, from this time onwards, those who came to use the Centre were never charged the full cost of the service, all places being subsidized by the charity. (*See* page 138.)

Through the 1980s, the Centre flourished and, as its reputation grew, so did the demand from the media, the public and healthcare professions for education and consultancy services. Help was requested with the design and building of other centres, support groups and hospital-based projects. These enquiries resulted in the setting up of many satellite holistic cancer support groups throughout Britain and the world. Penny and Pat personally helped initiate the establishment of centres in Italy, Sweden, Zimbabwe, South Africa, Hong Kong, Australia, New Zealand, America, and Japan. Christopher meanwhile took on the role of regularly visiting the 100 or so groups that had sprung up around Britain, helping to encourage, guide and support them in the healing work they were doing.

The most notable of the consultative projects in which the Centre was involved was the Hammersmith Project. This was instigated by Professor Karol Sikora, who had been impressed by the tremendous turnaround he had seen in the morale of his patients who were attending the Centre. He had also observed that some 37 per cent of his patients were already using some form of complementary help or another. After a long period of collaboration, Professor Sikora opened the Hammersmith Hospital Oncology Department Supportive Care Unit in 1991. Here, his department's patients could receive holistic therapies, support and counselling whilst undergoing conventional treatment of their illness. This unit continues to this day and, in 1999, won the Foundation for Integrated Medicine award for the best model of integrated healthcare practice in Britain.

## Troubled Times

However, despite all the very positive progress during the 1980s, there was an undercurrent of antagonism from within the fields of oncology and psycho-social oncology. In a televized discussion following the T.V. series, 'The Gentle Way With Cancer', Dr Walter Bodmer of the Imperial Cancer Research Fund, and Professor Tim McElwain of the Marsden Hospital, publicly challenged the heretical assertion being made by Penny and Alec that people with cancer could affect their prognosis, throwing down the gauntlet that they be allowed to research the Centre's results. In 1984, discussions began and protocols were agreed for the comparison of the survival and quality of life of patients with a primary diagnosis of breast cancer attending Bristol Cancer Help Centre with a control group of non-attenders.

Whilst the Centre's work and reputation was gathering immense momentum, and elsewhere barriers of mistrust within the medical profession were being melted away, the Institute of

Cancer Research, funded by the Imperial Cancer Research Fund and Cancer Research Council, were collecting data from Bristol. They were comparing this with the Cancer Registry's data on 'matched subjects' who had already died.

In 1990, two years into the five-year trial, the Studies Director, Professor Claire Chilvers, announced that the interim findings of the study were that people coming to Bristol were relapsing and dying more quickly than people who had had orthodox treatment alone. Rather than investigating these very unlikely statistics further, the cancer charities decided to call an immediate press conference to release these findings. The announcement made the nine o'clock news, and many thousands of people using the Bristol Approach heard that evening, in this shattering way, that it appeared they were actually putting themselves at serious risk by following the Bristol programme.

Within days, people stopped coming to Bristol, the donors stopped donating, staff were laid off, and collapse seemed inevitable. Had the statistics been less dramatic – or even if they had appeared to show that coming to Bristol made no difference at all – the Centre would probably have folded then and there. However, because the statistics were so outrageous, many doctors and scientists came to the Centre's rescue, quickly discovering a series of 'fatal flaws' within the studies' methodology. It became clear that those who had been studied from the Centre were a much younger group of women who were in fact much more ill than those with whom they had been compared. Also, no check had been made on the extent to which any of these 'Bristol subjects' had fully embarked upon the Bristol Approach: this meant that it was quite possible for somebody who had visited Bristol only once, without ever taking up any aspect of the approach, to be counted as a Bristol patient.

The study and its authors were discredited and, tragically, one of the instigators of the study, Professor McElwain, took his own life within weeks of the bitter and vitriolic aftermath of the débâcle. The damage did not stop there. Less than a year after this dreadful fight for the life of the Centre, Penny's own cancer recurred in her spine.

## Restoration

The women in the study suffered greatly, too, because during the fierce battle between Bristol and the cancer charities they were left unsupported by either agency and indeed they went on to play an extraordinarily heroic role in righting the wrong that had been done to Bristol's reputation. Spearheaded by Heather Goodare and Isla Bourke, the Bristol Survey Support Group was formed. Amazingly this group managed in April 1992 to get Channel 4 to publicize the story (in a programme called 'Cancer Positive' in the 'Free For All' consumer series), and they received apologies from heads of the cancer charities involved.

Furthermore, in April 1992, they initiated an investigation by the Charities Commission, which in January 1994 found the cancer charities guilty of inadequate supervision of the research. The Centre will be eternally indebted to these brave women who achieved much whilst the Centre clung to the rocks by its fingernails, running a very depleted service with a shoestring staff. During these hard times major efforts were made to repair the damage to the Centre's credibility, and under the direction of first Dr Michael Weir and then Dr Rosy Daniel, with a team of loyal and experienced therapists, the Centre went on to restore its reputation and, ultimately, to become even stronger than before.

Several things helped a great deal with this process. First of all, deeply disturbed by the incident and the threat to Bristol's existence, The Prince of Wales gave unstinting support, helping Bristol in any way he could to rebuild its network of friends and donors. He officially became Patron of the Centre in 1996. This vote of confidence boosted the morale of those of us working at the Centre enormously.

The other crucial factor that helped to rebuild the Centre was the rapid evolution of scientific evidence underpinning the approach, most particularly in the field of psycho-social oncology. Dr Stephen Greer showed how very much the survival of patients with fighting spirit is improved over those who become helpless and hopeless (*see* pages 42–3).[1] Added to this was the important work of Doctors Spiegel[2] and Fawzy-Fawzy,[3] who demonstrated the extended survival of people with cancer who attended support groups. The biggest help of all came from the newly emerging field of psychoneuroimmunology (PNI) which gave us an explanation for the mechanism through which both negative and positive emotional influences can affect healing and immune function (*see* pages 38–42).[4]

Simultaneously, research evidence was linking diet to cancer,[5] and vitamins and mineral supplementation to cancer prevention.[6] There were also many positive studies on the roles of complementary therapies in improving symptom control, toleration of treatments and the quality of life in people with cancer.[7] One particularly important study from Dr Leslie Walker showed improved survival in those who employed the practice of visualization during chemotherapy.[8]

The widespread dissemination of this research work through teaching and media activities during the 1990s led to the making of important documentaries on the role of PNI effects, headed by journalist Alison Delaney in Bristol, and to the inclusion of the Centre's teaching input in the 1998 Annual Conference of the World Health Organization on worldwide cancer strategy. Requests came in for contributions to many of the current teaching textbooks for oncologists. In fact the Bristol Cancer Help Centre's sphere of influence has become so large in the world of cancer medicine that Professor Karol Sikora, head of the Cancer Division of the World Health Organization, has called it the 'gold standard in complementary cancer care'. The Prince of Wales has described what a 'great pleasure it has been over the years to see how much the Bristol Cancer Help Centre has influenced the development of cancer medicine'.

It is certainly clear from the work of the Foundation for Integrated Medicine (initiated by The Prince of Wales), which aims to promote the development of integrated medical services in Britain, that far greater progress has been made towards this end in cancer medicine than in any other branch of medicine. I am quite sure that a great deal of this progress is owed to the influence of the Bristol Cancer Help Centre.

## Penny Brohn's Legacy

Now, at the beginning of the new millennium, the benefits of giving people self-help tools and support to deal with the impact of diagnosis and treatments are being recognized, and complementary supportive care is being incorporated into many cancer units and hospice services. Certainly Penny Brohn never dreamed that within 20 years of the Centre's founding in 1980 such a level of acceptance and integration would have occurred by the year 2000, and, if the present level of momentum and change continues, it seems highly likely that within the next ten years people with cancer will be able to experience not only toleration of, but encouragement of, their involvement in their recovery processes.

Penny herself lived with her cancer for 20 years from the time of her diagnosis. She died at home on 3 February 1999 with her now grown-up family around her. She was 'healed into her dying' by two of the Centre's healers, Janet Swan and Cynthia Evanson, and could not have made a more gracious and conscious departure from this world.

She proved to me beyond any shadow of doubt, her own complete conviction that cancer is a two-way process over which the individual can have a major influence. During those 20 years she had six recurrences of her cancer, which she met heroically on every occasion. After reacting each time with entirely appropriate fear and grief, she would come flying back with her own startling creativity, ingenuity, insight and wit, leaving those of us who supported and helped her breathless with admiration.

Her 20 years of living with breast cancer – a disease for which there is only a 50–60 per cent 5-year survival average – is utterly staggering. And Penny's story is only one of the many hundreds of remarkable achievements that have been made by people with cancer who have walked this path in Penny's footsteps. The Bristol Approach to Cancer is now her legacy. Her brilliant discoveries, and the many insights and therapeutic developments that have been made over the years at Bristol, continue to be passed on through the work of the Centre's expert therapy team and the quite exceptional current-day therapy programme at Bristol.

## The Best of Both Worlds

The first question many people who come to the Centre ask is, 'Can I use the Bristol Approach alongside orthodox medicine?'. The answer is a resounding 'Yes'. In fact integration of holistic and orthodox approaches is very likely to result in better treatment outcomes, reduced symptoms and side-effects of treatments, and overall a far greater sense of control and much improved quality of life. The majority of people who come to Bristol opt for this 'best of both worlds' approach, although some want to use holistic or alternative approaches only.

It is Bristol's policy to support each individual in the choices and decisions they make, and no pressure is placed on anybody to pursue any particular form or style of treatment, orthodox or complementary. Rather, the approach is to offer in-depth medical counselling, once the person has recovered from the shock of diagnosis, in order to make sure that the choices they are making are right for them. In fact, once time and unconditional support are given, and their fears are addressed, people often change their initial ideas about refusing treatment and accept conventional intervention.

## Medical Policy at Bristol

It is made absolutely clear to everyone coming to Bristol that the Cancer Help Centre is not a medical cancer treatment centre. The doctors at the Centre do not get involved in the medical management of cancer: this is left entirely to the individual's hospital team and GP, although the Centre's doctors correspond with the GP and consultants of people attending the courses. The Centre's doctors are also able to talk to the person's medical team if required, and any omission or error that might be spotted in an individual's overall medical management is reported to the medical team involved, as are any new medical developments or symptoms that may arise while the person is staying at Bristol. In cases of emergency, Centre staff will arrange for treatment or admission to a hospital locally, or transport home if necessary. The Centre has 24-hour medical cover whilst there are people in residence.

The Centre does not hold any medical drugs or equipment on the premises, and visitors must therefore bring their medication and dressings with them. To make this crystal clear, those using the Centre are required to sign an indemnity form confirming that they understand Bristol is not a medical treatment centre and does not undertake medical responsibility for their overall care.

There is no attempt by the Centre's therapy team to 'manage' those who come on the programmes, as the self-management aspect of the Bristol approach is seen as pivotal in the recovery process. So whilst education, choices, guidance, therapy and support are given, the combination of therapies and self-help techniques chosen by the client for continuation at home is entirely individual; control and responsibility is entirely in their hands.

The Bristol Approach has never claimed to be a cure for cancer. Rather it offers individuals access to the many therapies and ideas that might help to reduce the severity of symptoms, improve outcomes from treatments, enhance quality of life and mental state, and, possibly, affect prognosis or survival. People are shown the evidence base that indicates that lifting oneself out of depressed or hopeless states of mind, getting support, and using self-help techniques have all been shown to improve prognosis.

## The Centre's Therapeutic Process

The therapeutic process at Bristol Cancer Help Centre has two main aims:

1. To help people with cancer to deal with their diagnosis and treatment, and to assist them in finding all possible forms of medical, complementary and alternative help to treat the cancer and its symptoms.

2. To help promote the health of people with cancer in the presence of their illness.

The first aim, of helping people to deal with the cancer itself, involves giving:

- Support and care to help people recover from the diagnosis of cancer (at all stages that cancer is diagnosed).
- Medical counselling to help people make difficult medical decisions.
- Help in coping with the rigours of treatment.
- Help in achieving symptom control both from the cancer itself and from the side-effects of treatment.
- Advice about complementary and alternative treatments for cancer.

The second aim, of helping to promote health in the presence of illness, is achieved by helping clients to:

- Develop a nurturing, responsible and protective relationship with themselves.
- Establish healthy eating patterns.
- Reduce stress.
- Exercise.
- Explore personal spirituality.
- Attain personal empowerment.
- Re-establish meaningful core values.
- Realign lifestyle to reflect core values.
- Achieve self-expression and promote their own creativity.
- Achieve creative, self-expressive, meaningful and purposeful activity.

In practice, these processes go on simultaneously throughout the Centre's programme, and aspects of the two main aims are contained within the roles of all therapists at the Centre.

---

### Referrals

Currently only 10 per cent of Bristol clients are referred by their doctors, nurses and social workers. Most people come to Bristol through self-referral, having heard about the Centre by word of mouth or through the media.

---

# 2

# *Science and the Holistic Approach*

The word 'holistic', which derives from the Greek word *holos* (meaning 'whole'), describes the concept that a whole is greater than the sum of its parts. The holistic approach to health therefore involves careful consideration of the state of the whole person, i.e. viewing our health, or illness, as the result of interacting influences of mind, body and spirit, and the environment in which we live. The word itself conveys not only a sense of the interconnectedness of mind, body and spirit but the profound way in which we are interconnected with each other and all that is around us.

## The Holistic Model

In the West, the conventional model of medicine is reductionistic, or mechanistic. The body is viewed as a machine, and when this machine malfunctions the focus is entirely on the part of the machine that has failed. In other words, nine times out of ten modern medicine looks at the symptoms, not at the conditions in which the illness has arisen; it looks at tissues, cells, DNA, and biochemistry, not at the person as a whole. And although this approach has resulted in some brilliant discoveries, and made many technical solutions possible, it also creates a culture in which the patient is made to feel alienated, helpless and fearful.

What is being neglected in this model is the individual's intuitive understanding of where an illness may have come from. Often, insufficient care and thought is given to what is needed through the process of treatment; and, most important of all, the individual's own resources – mental, physical and spiritual – are not being utilized in the recovery process. People often say they feel that the doctor's focus is not on them but on the illness they present, and that they find this a frightening process; they feel bereft and abandoned with their feelings, and feel that their own involvement and insight into their illness or problem is being overlooked.

In taking an holistic approach we start from the other perspective. Each person is seen as the greatest expert on themselves, and it is acknowledged that many important factors that affect health are within that person's control: do we nourish, care for and protect ourselves from destructive influences, or do we chronically abandon, neglect or even abuse ourselves? In what way are our relationships or our environment affecting us? Or, at an even more profound level, what is going on in our relationship with life itself? Have we lost our joy in living – our sense of meaning, purpose and fulfilment? Has our personal spirit become crushed or dispirited? In the holistic model we ask all these questions as well as helping individuals to become aware of the state of their lives, their bodies, minds and spirit so that gradually a gentle and exciting restoration and rebalancing process can occur.

This may at first sound a bit odd to those of us who have been brought up in the West, for we have been educated to believe that there are always experts and doctors who will know how we function and who will make us better if things go wrong. So it might help to illustrate the way in which the holistic model works by using the analogy of an overgrown garden. If you take on a property whose garden has been neglected for many years, the first thing you will do is cut down and dig out all the brambles and weeds, which are choking the plants and trees, and have a big bonfire. Then, rather than digging up the whole garden, you will (if you are a good gardener) wait to see what new life begins to emerge. You will nurture this new life as it appears through the first year, all the time assessing what is healthy and strong. After a year or so you may choose to start moving plants, adding new ones or doing earthworks to create more interest and excitement.

This is exactly what it is like working with the holistic approach. Working holistically towards promoting health and well-being can be seen as a three-stage process:

1. First, we help individuals to look at what aspects of their lifestyle are choking their life-force and draining their energy or burdening, depressing or stressing them.

2. Then we help them to identify and gently remove these destructive factors from their lives.

3. Finally we look for the emerging life and energy, nourishing and encouraging this new 'aliveness' until the individual is strong and vital.

In each one of us there is more that is basically right than wrong. So the holistic approach involves recognizing and nurturing the parts of ourselves that are absolutely fine and just need a little 'light of day' to thrive.

I was devastated by the secondary diagnosis – completely destroyed. I went through the conventional treatment very successfully but realized that this was a warning I could not ignore. I needed to take a long hard look at my lifestyle – the hours I was working, the stress of my job, the lack of sleep, and the junk food – and make some dramatic changes for the future.

*Angela Burns: living with secondary*
*breast cancer, first diagnosed in 1991*

As we start becoming involved in the things that really nourish us and enable us to express ourselves, our energy levels rise rapidly; and as therapists encourage individuals to choose and enhance the areas in their lives about which they are really passionate and excited, the mind and spirit become progressively stronger, with the body following close behind. This sounds simple, but of course the difficulty and skill in making this happen is in the first part of the process – in recognizing and getting ourselves unhooked from the rigid patterns and behaviours that drain us of our vital energy.

The holistic approach concentrates on five key elements:

1. Health, rather than illness.
2. Interconnectedness of mind, body and spirit.
3. Our relationship with ourselves.
4. Carers and medics honouring individual needs.
5. Nutrition and exercise.

## 1. Health rather than illness

This means promoting health by focusing on what is right, rather than what is wrong, with us, and doing this in the knowledge that there is always something that can be done to improve well-being and quality of life.

## 2. Interconnectedness of mind, body and spirit

These three aspects of ourselves are not independent. In other words, problems that affect any one of them will also affect the others. Conversely therapy that is concentrated on any one of these levels will benefit the others.

This means that in assessing an individual's state the key imperatives are to establish the state of the individual's spirit and will to live. Has the person become crushed, disillusioned and dispirited, bereft of spiritual nourishment? Or is the person aware of the needs of their soul or spirit, and able to get these needs met? All those involved in medicine know that if an individual's spirit has been broken and the will to live has gone, there is no medicine, orthodox or complementary, that will get them well again.

Next we need to look at the current and long-term emotional state of the individual, and ask the important question, 'Is the individual able to express his or her emotions. In Britain we have a great tendency to labour under the effects of the 'stiff upper lip' syndrome, and to place great importance on being nice and polite. In the world of holistic medicine there is an adage that 'what the mind represses the body expresses'. Emotions that are denied a means of outward expression over a long period do not simply disappear; rather they are expressed in the body, ultimately causing havoc with our physiology. If we cannot speak and act honestly, letting other people know how we feel, our sense of isolation and alienation will increase.

In classical Chinese medicine, different organs of the body are considered to be affected by different emotions. This is often borne out in psychotherapeutic practice when skilled therapists and the individuals involved 'crack the code', releasing the emotional block in the body, and resulting in rapid resolution of physical symptoms. Helping individuals to become aware of the emotions they are repressing, and promoting emotional expression on a regular basis, are of key importance in the holistic approach and can make a huge difference to health.

I was bottling everything up all the time, and then finally I realized that this was one of my biggest problems and it was causing me a lot of trouble. I found different ways to release all this tension, and the first obvious thing was to have a good cry – it was amazing how good it made me feel afterwards. The other thing I found was singing at the top of my voice in the car (which I never used to do) – and I've got a terrible voice! I just felt more and more relaxed as time went on, and felt much better in myself.

*Reg Flower: living with secondary melanoma,*
*first diagnosed in 1981*

We must also look at an individual's underlying beliefs and attitudes, and consider how these may be governing behaviour, causing that person to stress or drain themselves or limit their achievement.

> I realized that I really had to make life changes. I'd always been a 'yes' person. People would phone me up all hours of the day and night, and 'Yes, Jenny would do it', even if nobody else would. I couldn't say no to people. Afterwards I'd put the phone down and wish I'd thought about it. I realized that I'd never put myself first – I was always worrying about other people.
>
> *Jenny Jackson: living with liver cancer,*
> *first diagnosed in 1987*

If we believe that we are hopeless, bad, or unlovable, and that we must constantly prove or modify ourselves to earn the respect and love of others, we are likely to put ourselves continuously under terrible pressure and wear ourselves to a frazzle in the process. We may have many aspects, or 'sub-personalities', to our nature, and our lives may be dominated or sabotaged by an extremely critical, pushy, demanding or punishing aspect of ourselves which does not allow the gentler, more creative aspects of our nature to emerge. Recognizing these patterns, and allowing our 'slave driver' sub-personality to take a prolonged holiday is the key step in the recovery process.

The best way to make the mind–body connection work to optimize health is to discover what really brings us alive and excites us the most. Lawrence LeShan, the 'grandfather' of the holistic approach, has described this as finding the way for each individual to 'sing their own song'. It means being so involved in things that excite you that when you go to bed each night you feel like a child on Christmas Eve. Of course, it is hard to imagine anyone feeling like this all the time, but certainly many of us have resigned ourselves to living in a very grey, compromised state where almost nothing we do really engages or excites us. This is not a good state for the long-term health of the body.

## 3. Our relationship with ourselves

In looking at our relationships with ourselves, with others, and with life itself, the emphasis is on seeking to achieve optimum balance. In parts of the East this balance is called 'living in the Tao'. What is universally discovered by people as they move closer and closer to this state of balance is that their sense of the interconnectedness of life, their personal intuition and understanding, their sense of inner knowing, and the occurrence of synchronistic or significant coincidences in their lives, becomes very heightened.

> Ten years ago, perhaps, it was the material things that were of value to me – power of impression, prestige. But nowadays it's my close friends, it's nature (I find a lot of strength in nature), it's my family. We live in the woods, and I don't have a rush, rush, rush lifestyle as I did previously. I think it has been very healing.
>
> *Zoe Lindgren: living with lung secondaries of*
> *breast cancer, first diagnosed in 1988*

Contained within this principle is the emphasis placed on each individual's formation of a dynamic, responsible, loving relationship with themselves and their health. Individuals are urged to become aware of how they are damaging or promoting their health; they are encouraged to give up the passive assumption that they can take liberties with their health and expect others to put it right. This type of truly healthy relationship with oneself should not be confused with becoming over responsible, neurotic or self-blaming. Essentially it must begin from wherever you are, without any unhelpful self-judgement, so that you can see what may be achieved by starting to take better care of yourself.

This effectively means helping individuals to place themselves in the driving seat, to take control and become active partners in the management and promotion of their own health. It is important to realize straight away, though, that for many of us self-help is not possible until we are far stronger, so support and often therapeutic help are needed to enable us to make the first steps towards true health. Usually the negative holding patterns that keep us locked in either self-destructive or non-expressive lifestyles are based on fear and loneliness, or lack of belief in ourselves or the possibility that life will ever get any better. Usually an injection of love, support, energy and encouragement is required to change this. Then, once some headway has been made, it is possible for the individual to sustain and build on this progress themselves.

In taking this active approach to health, people become much more assertive in medical situations, seeing themselves as active partners with the medical personnel and not purely passive, dependent recipients of medical advice and care. Overall the aim is to develop an active 'fighting spirit' that will enable you to take an active role and so lift yourself out of the state of hopelessness/helplessness and depression. More fundamentally this means changing your attitude to life and learning to put yourself and your needs first.

Learning to put yourself first depends upon building your self-esteem and assertiveness and learning to recognize and honour your needs. It means developing a much more tender and caring relationship with yourself, and drawing up new boundaries to protect your health and energy. This often means quite simply learning to say 'no' to the demands and expectations of others. Healthcare professionals have a very significant role to play here in promoting rather than discouraging active involvement of individuals in their health care, as this can make a considerable difference to outcome, and to the sense of control that their patients feel. It has even been shown that 'difficult' patients do better and live longer.

## 4. Carers and medics honouring individual needs

The fourth element of the holistic approach involves those in the medical or caring role honouring and working with the individual's own values, wisdom and intuition, taking note of what they know and feel about themselves.

All of us have a great deal of information about ourselves; and we also have an inner voice, which speaks wisely to us if only we quieten down enough to hear it (and take heed of it when we do hear it). Many of us hear our inner voice giving us advice – for example, 'don't buy that car' or 'don't get involved in that relationship' – but often we completely ignore or over-ride it, and must then spend years getting out of a situation that we could have avoided if only we'd listened to that intuitive part of ourselves – that inner voice. Often this happens because we have listened only to the more pushy or fear-driven aspect of ourselves, or deferred to other people's judgement, giving our power away in the process. We are then acting on the basis of what we think others expect of us, and in doing this we lose our own authenticity and our sense of being 'true to ourselves'.

This inner voice has a very important part to play when we are ill, for if we can find and listen to that voice, or take notice of our higher selves, we can often attain a profound understanding of the real nature of our problem and what we need in order to help put things right. This part of us may reveal itself in symbols, dreams, or in recurring patterns of behaviour or events. At first we may need the skill of a transpersonal counsellor to help us recognize and understand the language of our inner voice. Transpersonal counselling aims to restore the balance between the various elements of the personality and the psyche. When one starts to do this on a regular basis, the humour, wisdom and rewards can be quite wonderful, and the insights gained can provide the foundations for a much more solid and happy life.

> I discovered an inner life that I certainly didn't know I had, and certainly wasn't nurturing, and I discovered how valu-

able and healing that was. I learned to be still and listen to my body's needs. I've changed my life quite radically. I've given up full-time work (I'm fortunate in being able to do a variety of paid and unpaid part-time work), I have more leisure time – and a lot more fun!

*Angela Burns: living with secondary*
*breast cancer, first diagnosed in 1991*

## 5. Nutrition and exercise

In taking the holistic approach to health we must also address the question of our nutritional state, fitness, and the oxygenation of our tissues.

Degenerative diseases thrive in anaerobic, sugary, fatty conditions. So when we don't eat well, don't exercise, and don't breathe properly, our tissues become deoxygenized and de-energized, providing the ideal environment for calcification, fat deposition, sclerosis and carcinogenesis to occur. The absence of sufficient vegetable and fruit material in our diets puts us at further risk, particularly of cancer. The progressive reduction in our energy levels is reflected in our mental state, which also becomes sluggish and defeated, making it harder to tackle negative, self-destructive cycles of behaviour.

In short, the holistic approach to health enables us not only to create individually tailored programmes of therapy, support, healing, and complementary and orthodox medicine, but to enhance the effectiveness of any therapy or treatment by helping individuals to prepare themselves to receive treatment, to cope with the treatment itself, and to work towards recovering their health.

## The Energy System of the Body

There is another way of looking at how lifestyle, mental state, and therapeutic intervention interact. In all the ancient models of health and medicine from the East, and in the European system of homoeopathic medicine, the underlying concept is that the overall state of the body and mind is linked to energy levels or vitality. In other words, the body has an inherent, underlying energy force that affects, and is affected by, everything else.

In the acupuncture system, from China, this fundamental energy of our system is called *chi*. In shiatsu, from Japan, it is called *ki*. In the Indian yogic tradition it is called prana, and in homoeopathy it is called 'the vital force'. In the West we might also call it our vitality or *joie de vivre*. What is clear is that in all these systems of medicine, the traditional practitioner looks at the underlying energy state of the body – whether it is raised or lowered, flowing or stagnant, in or out of balance – rather than looking at the organs and tissues of the body.

Nowadays, with high-technology photographic techniques we can actually see the energy field of the body and begin to visualize for ourselves the subtle energy systems on which Oriental and homoeopathic medicine is based. With new bio-energy measuring and treatment devices, such as the Russian 'Kosmed', or 'Scenar' device, we can actually measure the body's energy levels and treat them simultaneously. It is extremely interesting to note that through modern physics we know categorically that all matter is fundamentally made of energy. It says much about the sensitivity and consciousness of our ancestors that they were so easily able to detect, assess and rebalance, the subtle energies of the body.

## The energy model

It can be helpful to imagine that all of us have a spectrum of possible energy or vitality from 0 to 100 per cent, and that when we are born we are usually at the highest energy level (*see* page 28) In the West, owing to a combination of poor diet, alcohol, cigarettes, stress, over-work, over-stimulation and sedentary lifestyle, most of us are running at only half our potential energy.

The most common complaint in the majority of GP surgeries is the TATT syndrome (feeling tired all the time). It is clear that

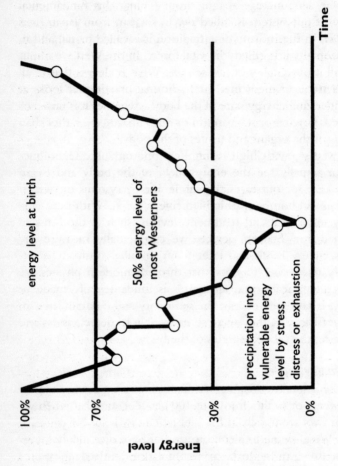

The energy model. Energy plummets as health deteriorates, and rises again as health is improved through therapy and self-help.

in the West many of us are suffering from a serious depletion of our vital force. At around the 50 per cent energy level we may become susceptible to colds and influenza and minor ailments, but if our vital energy goes still lower, through an excessive period of overwork or upset, shock, disappointment or infection, we can be taken below a critical level of, say, 30 per cent.

Below this critical point, any potential problem to which we are innately susceptible – whether it is schizophrenia, asthma, cancer or anything else – becomes far more likely to manifest itself. When the condition or problem is perceived by us to be an extremely serious one, such as cancer, the shock of the diagnosis lowers the energy levels further, and conventional treatment lowers them further again, leaving the individual absolutely floored. If at this point it is suggested that all you need to do is completely reappraise your lifestyle, meditate twice a day, and totally change your diet, this can be the final straw, propelling your energy levels to rock bottom. After all, if you really have to change all that, can life still be worth living?

The real problem here is that when the *chi* or vitality drops below this critical level, the state of mind also changes. People become depressed; they feel out of control and have much higher fear levels; they lose self-esteem; they find it hard to sleep, and are more likely to use drugs, alcohol, tobacco, or misuse food, or to indulge in other addictive or compulsive behaviours in an effort to give their energy and mental state a boost. In the long run, of course, these tactics inevitably worsen the situation by increasing toxicity in the body and reducing energy levels still further.

Most crucially of all, low energy levels can engender demotivation and even loss of the will to live. In this low-energy state, self-help is almost completely impossible or, worse still, counterproductive: if individuals are set the task of embarking upon a self-help programme when they are too low, tired or vulnerable to undertake it, they are likely to feel defeated by it. Their sense of failure and self-criticism will then be exacerbated by

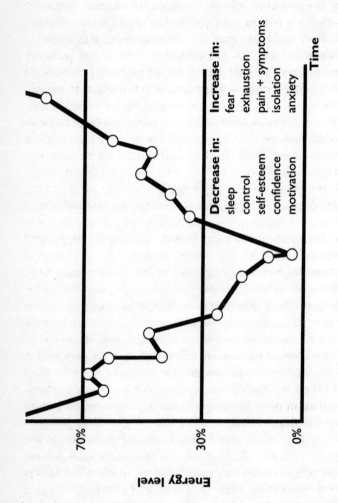

**Energy level**

70%

30%

0%

**Decrease in:**
sleep
control
self-esteem
confidence
motivation

**Increase in:**
fear
exhaustion
pain + symptoms
isolation
anxiety

Time

*The effect on the individual's state of mind when the energy level falls below the critical 30% level.*

their knowledge that they could be doing something to help themselves but are incapable of doing it. In fact the feeling that self-help is impossibly difficult is one of the clearest diagnostic indicators that a person's energy level is critically low. We can find ourselves in this low-energy state even when we are not ill at all. Much of the time we know that we would feel far better if we were able to go to the gym, or have a swim, meditate or do some yoga, but often our energy is too low for us to be able to do this.

It is vitally important, therefore, to make an accurate assessment of the current energy level. When energy levels are too low to facilitate self-help, therapeutic help is in the first instance necessary to raise the energy level. The therapies that will activate the process of increasing energy are spiritual healing and the energy medicines of shiatsu, acupuncture and homoeopathy. It is also important in this phase to have therapies that reduce fear levels and promote relaxation. Massage and aromatherapy, and group sessions in which the person is encouraged to off-load emotion, and in which he or she can be led through relaxation, meditation and visualization practices by an experienced facilitator, also give the individual immediate help.

When people are in this low state the first key to recovery is in being able to 'let go' and allow themselves to receive help and energy input. This is difficult for many people who find it hard to relinquish control – people who always give rather than receive. Often we seem to need active permission to be tired, sick or fed up in order that others may help. Getting the necessary help will depend on our being able to give clear messages to our therapists and supporters that we have become temporarily depleted and are in need of active support. Allowing this input of help and energy to take place can often be the first step towards catalysing the overall healing a person needs.

In this low-energy phase spiritual healing is wonderful, which is why healing is the cornerstone of the work at the Bristol Cancer Help Centre. The great beauty of spiritual healing is that you do not have to think about it, talk about it, or do anything at all. All that is necessary is for you to be there in a receptive mode, literally soaking up the energy that is being channelled to you by the healer who acts almost like a jump lead, recharging your battery.

A good way to illustrate what happens during healing is to compare the person to a boat in the harbour when the tide has gone out: the boat might be an extremely well-made, elegant yacht, but in the low-tide conditions it can do nothing but lie on the sand, unable to go anywhere at all. Six hours later, when the tide has come in, that same boat could sail to South America. This is what it is like for the individual whose *chi* or energy is low but then receives healing. Before healing they may feel completely floored, like the stranded yacht; but afterwards they feel revitalized, and able to take charge of their situation. Their energy level has been restored to above the critical 30 per cent line, enabling them to become actively involved and motivated in promoting their own health.

The pitfall at this point is of course that now that their energy has returned, people immediately want to go back to their old lifestyle and patterns of behaviour, making up for all the time they have lost being ill and repaying what they perceive to be their debt to those who looked after them. So the second key here is for people to learn the absolutely vital importance of putting themselves first: reorganizing their priorities and values in life around meeting their own needs. At this stage it is important to conserve this precious new energy and go on to increase it through self-help practices.

Self-help will typically involve a combination of healthy diet, relaxation, meditation, visualization, exercise, and becoming involved with whatever is really exciting and inspiring. In a way, we could say that during therapy the therapist sets an example of the kind of tender loving care one deserves and, once you move into the self-help phase, then it is your job to continue to give yourself the same level of protective nurturing and care. In other

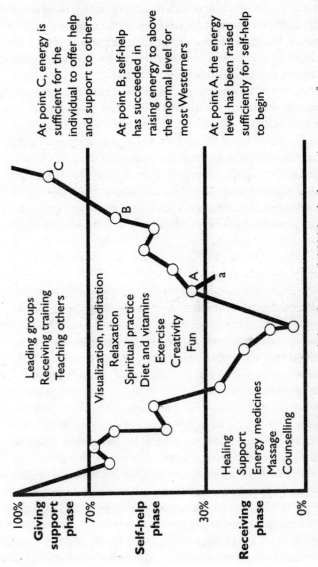

100%

**Giving support phase**

70%

**Self-help phase**

30%

**Receiving phase**

0%

Leading groups
Receiving training
Teaching others

Visualization, meditation
Relaxation
Spiritual practice
Diet and vitamins
Exercise
Creativity
Fun

Healing
Support
Energy medicines
Massage
Counselling

At point C, energy is sufficient for the individual to offer help and support to others

At point B, self-help has succeeded in raising energy to above the normal level for most Westerners

At point A, the energy level has been raised sufficiently for self-help to begin

*The phases of recovery. When energy is below the critical 30% level, therapy is necessary for the process of recovery to begin. Self-help must then be instigated to ensure that energy does not fall below the critical level again (a), and that the recovery process continues.*

words, therapy provides you with a new template on which you can model a different sort of relationship with yourself.

Organizing life around your own needs may at first seem self-ish, but in fact, as people become stronger, healthier, happier, and more truly themselves, the positive effect of this spreads out to the rest of their family, friends and colleagues. They are not being martyrs any more, sacrificing themselves to the needs of others and wondering why they are not appreciated. More than this, their giving to those around them becomes far less condi-tional, and they find that they can love more fully. This is because, of course, people cannot give from the empty place that chronically abandoning themselves creates. Sometimes it becomes apparent that what may have looked, in the past, like giving may actually have been taking at the energetic or emo-tional level.

## The energy around us

Another facet of the energy model is the question of how the energies of others affect us. It is very interesting to note that quite often people with cancer are what could be called 'ener-gy chameleons' or 'symptom carriers'. They tend to take on or soak up the difficult energies and emotions that surround them in an attempt to harmonize and bring peace to their situation. They are often not aware of what is their own and what is another's emotion or energy, and do not realize what they are taking on. It is often quite diagnostic that the minute these peo-ple are in natural surroundings they feel better, as they become affected by the healthy energy systems of plants and trees, and begin to harmonize and resonate with these refreshing energies. Such people are called 'sensitives' and can also be affected quite markedly by 'electrical environments', earth energies, or diffi-cult individuals whose energies they pick up.

During the process of becoming aware of the energy state of body, mind and spirit in different situations it can be help-ful for individuals to notice the way they feel in different environments, really watching for situations in which their energy rises and those in which their energy drops. This can lead to some very surprising discoveries because, often, the very situations or people we have always considered to be central to our well-being or nourishment can turn out to be the ones that are draining us the most – particularly when those

---

### Making time for yourself

Whether it is overwork, chronic busyness or over-giving that is the problem there is often a pressing need to timetable space for ourselves into our lifestyle. It is important to take this time alone so that we can digest and process what has been happening to us, andallow our nervous system and mind to be calmed so that re-equilibration of our energies and self-healing can begin.

We could look at this energy equation in budgetary terms, and ask ourselves, 'How am I spending my energy, where is it all going, and is this right?' And, more importantly, 'How do I build my energy, and am I spending more than I am generating?'

Some people are very resistant to taking restorative time on their own because they are terrified of being with themselves, usually because of overwhelming feelings of loneliness or other unnamed fears. This can also be a block to the learning of meditation – the fear that the moment one stops doing or being outwardly focused the feelings inside will be unbearable. In both cases a counsellor can help us negotiate our way into our inner space, and thus to begin our new inner life. Once this process has begun the relief is enormous. The constant pressure and drive to keep moving is released, and true rest and healing becomes possible.

relationships or commitments are based on fear or duty. Once you have gained these insights you can – with support and help, often from counsellors – start to make the appropriate changes or, at the very least, learn how to protect yourself if change is too difficult.

## The Therapeutic Ethos

Within the holistic approach the client's own assessment of their needs, and the choices they wish to make with regard to their health care, are considered to be of paramount importance. Individuals are therefore provided with the information necessary for them to make informed choices. This gives people a strong sense of validation of their own knowledge of themselves, and creates a very powerful therapeutic alliance with those caring for them.

Holistic practitioners place great emphasis upon the therapeutic relationship that they themselves have with the client, and also on the relationships between clients involved in group therapy as well as those between the members of the client's family and support network. The power of these relationships in the overall healing process is pivotal. The key role of the holistic practitioner is to ensure that the individual has sufficient time, understanding, care and encouragement, without prescription, to become fully aware of their own feelings, needs and therapeutic priorities, and ultimately their goals. In group therapy, it is the creation of boundaries and a sense of safety and trust that are especially important.

The therapeutic environment is an important factor within the holistic approach. Great emphasis is placed on beauty, tranquillity, comfort, emotional/spiritual safety, which together contribute to the accumulation of a palpable 'healing atmosphere' in places where a great deal of healing work is done. (This is often remarked upon by individuals entering Bristol Cancer Help Centre and other healing centres.)

## Conscious Dying and Spiritual Growth

Within the holistic philosophy, death is seen as a transition and not a failure, as a natural and inevitable part of life. This means that within the holistic approach, the individual who is approaching death is helped to become less fearful of it, and therefore to embrace it rather than reject it. Even if an individual is not healed physically, he or she may become healed at the mental and spiritual level, and may therefore be able to approach death more consciously in a state of peace with themselves and others, rather than going towards it in a state of fear, depression and confusion.

Overall, working with the holistic approach enables individuals to become involved in their conscious spiritual evolution through processes that revolve largely around the growth of their self-love, self-esteem and self-acceptance. It also involves recognition of the power of their creative will or consciousness to affect reality, and the discovery that help is also available from many sources around them socially and professionally, and from 'higher' or universal sources if they are prepared to ask for and receive it.

## The Scientific Evidence

The key questions for people with cancer and healthcare professionals are, what evidence is there that getting involved with our health makes any difference at all? What evidence is there that the mind, body and spirit are connected, or that expressing our emotions makes a difference to our health? How do we know that reducing our stress levels and getting ourselves involved in activities that fulfil us promote health and healing?

The holistic approach to health was developed intuitively over many centuries, and long pre-dates the existence of science. But in the past 50 years there has been a very rapid evolution in scientific understanding of the mechanisms involved in the holistic approach – from the role of diet in health to the crucial study of mind–body connections. This has been accelerated particularly in the last two decades with the development of the science of psychoneuroimmunology (PNI), which looks at how positive and negative states of mind affect tissue functioning in the body, and, most importantly, how these affect our immune system and our ability to resist and recover from illness.

## *Advances through psychoneuroimmunology (PNI)*

Since the early 1980s the discoveries made in the field of PNI have completely revolutionized our understanding of mind–body interaction. Previously the nervous system was thought of as separate from the body, with any interaction being mediated via the nerves and the neurotransmitters secreted at the nerve endings. However, the new scientists, most notably Dr Candace Pert,[8] have made us aware of a far more subtle and complex level of connection between the mind and the body. This has been made possible through their discovery of a vast family of tiny messenger chemicals – neuropeptides – which Dr Pert has called 'the molecules of emotion'. This started with her discovery of a receptor in the brain for an opiate-like substance, and shortly after this the actual substance itself was discovered; this substance was called enkephalin or endorphin.

The discovery that the brain made its own morphine-like compound started a great race to search for other messenger substances like this one; as a result, over 200 messenger chemicals, which are secreted by the brain and the tissues of the body, have been found. There are receptors for these neuropeptides, or informational substances, on all the tissues of the body, and when these molecules interact with the receptors they affect the cells' functioning either by activating the cells or by slowing down or deactivating them.

These neuropeptide molecules being secreted by both brain and body tissues provide an intricate two-way communication system. This discovery has led us to the profound realization that the intelligence and memory of the human being is not confined to the brain: our tissues themselves are intelligent, and even the immune system has the capacity for memory. It was this discovery by Dr Robert Ader in laboratory experiments with rats that propelled the field forward very rapidly.[9] He found that rats given saccharine combined with an immunosuppressant drug suffered severe depressions in their immune function when they were later fed saccharine alone. This demonstrated that the taste of the saccharine triggered the memory of the previously experienced immune response via mind–body connections, and, in many cases, a fatal depression of the rats' immune function.

This laboratory observation opened up the way for in-depth study of the human immune system, and particularly the effect of both positive and negative emotional states, memories and associations, made passively or actively, on the functioning of immune tissues. What has been shown is that the neuropeptides that are secreted during persistent states of depression, stress or distress actually depress the tissue functioning, and that, conversely, relaxation and positive imagery can boost immune function. It is very likely that it is this underlying mechanism that causes the mind–body reactions that people have witnessed for centuries – such as the onset of a hay-fever attack in midwinter in a hay-fever sufferer watching a film of meadows full of flowers, or the death of a healthy old person within weeks of their beloved spouse dying, once their reason for living has gone. In fact, since the naming of this field of PNI, it has become clear that it is not only immune tissue that is affected by the state of mind: the level of oxygen uptake of red blood cells, for example, is also affected by state of mind (again, the levels being lower in the depressed and/or stressed person).

These PNI processes are likely to be vitally important in cancer and many other illnesses because healthy, active immune cells recognize abnormal or infected cells and destroy them by attacking and engulfing them. It has been demonstrated quite clearly that in the person who is stressed, lonely and depressed, or unhappy, and in whom emotional expression is repressed, the immune blood cells multiply less fast, and the activities of the cells that do get made can be depressed in their activity by up to 50 per cent. Those with cancer who are isolated and socially disadvantaged have a worse prognosis than those from higher socio-economic groups. Through PNI, we can now see that when we are excited and happy and feeling loved or loving, our tissue and immune function increases dramatically.[11] And so we have a picture showing that just as a plant wilts when deprived of sunlight and water, so the body's tissues become compromised in their functioning as the spirit of an individual is deprived of love, excitement and satisfaction.

We can see immediately that in working to improve our health there is an absolute imperative to remove ourselves from constant stress, arousal and depression cycles. This can be helped immensely through the processes of relaxation and meditation. We can also help to free ourselves from chronically depressed states of mind and unexpressed emotion by using counselling and group therapy. It is even better to generate positive states of mind by getting actively involved in whatever inspires us so that our immune cells and tissues function optimally.

## The effects of stress on the body

Over the years our understanding of the effects of stress on the body has grown. The body's response to fear or threat is 'fight or flight'. A reaction of stress or fear involves the prioritization of resources in the body to the brain and muscles, so that we can think and then decide to run or fight. This happens at the expense of the housekeeping functions of the body, such as digestion, absorption, growth, healing, immunity and repair, all of which are put on hold whilst we are dealing with the perceived threat – real or imaginary, present or remembered. Thus our healing and homoeostatic mechanisms are greatly compromised when we are frightened or stressed.

We are designed to recover and rebalance ourselves from states of fear, moving back from this high level of sympathetic nervous system arousal into predominantly parasympathetic nervous system activity associated with relaxation, where the reverse process takes place. In this state the body's housekeeping functions are prioritized, and blood-flow and resources are directed to the digestion and repair functions rather than the brain and muscles.

We can easily identify this state as the more drowsy, lethargic feeling we get after eating – if we allow ourselves the time to relax and digest our food, that is. Imagine that, rather like the shape of an infinity sign, we are equipped to flow outwards into crisis and arousal, but then back in an equal and opposite direction so that the restoration, growth and healing processes can occur.

The big problem for many of us in the West is that we stay in the outer loop permanently, being stressed, stimulated and threatened much of the time. We often try to combat our stress by further stimulation, avoiding the process of relaxation because of the fear of facing how we actually feel inside if we slow down. In this state of chronic stress our immune system becomes severely compromised and our resistance to disease is markedly reduced. This reduction in the rate at which the immune cells multiply (*see* page 40) is a fundamental neuro-endocrine response of the body, which is mediated largely through activation of our adrenal glands. Our understanding has been that this was owed to the direct effects of adrenaline, noradrenaline and cortisol – the body's stress chemicals – and the natural stress steroid produced by the adrenal gland.

There are many other physiological effects of stress. For example, blood cholesterol levels go up; we lose calcium out of the bones; muscles become tense, and our guts do not work properly, giving rise to bowel problems and poor digestion. Even if we are eating high-quality food we are not getting the full benefit from it, and thus our ability to grow, repair our tissues or fight disease properly are diminished through the lack of nutrients. It becomes easy to see why in the West we are so vulnerable to many degenerative diseases, and to see how the mental state of fearfulness not only disturbs us emotionally, but severely compromises the body's ability to heal.

A great number of the holistic and self-help therapies, such as relaxation, meditation, massage, and counselling, reduce fear and anxiety, helping to establish predominantly parasympathetic self-healing states within the body.

## *The effect of depression on survival*

Scientists have been documenting PNI effects in people with cancer for years without understanding the mechanisms. The studies have involved looking at how the 'coping style' of people with a cancer diagnosis affects their survival rate. This pioneering work was done by Doctors Greer and Pettingale at the Marsden Hospital in the 1970s; in observing people with cancer they realized that individual survival patterns differed considerably, and that these patterns could be associated with the individual's initial reaction to the diagnosis.[1]

Greer and Pettingale described the different coping styles they were witnessing as 'fighting spirit', 'denial', 'stoic acceptance or fatalism', and 'helplessness and hopelessness or anxious preoccupation'. They assessed the psychological reaction of a group of women diagnosed with breast cancer – making their assessment within days of the diagnosis being made – and then followed them for 15 years, comparing the survival rates of the women with different coping styles. Even they were surprised by the results.

At 13 years into the study, 80 per cent of those that had started with fighting spirit were still alive, and 50 per cent of the deniers were still alive, but only 30 per cent of the stoics and 20 per cent of the helpless and hopeless had survived. Most significant of all, 80 per cent of those that became helpless and hopeless died within two years of receiving their diagnosis. (And this in a disease that has an average 5-year survival rate of 50 per cent.) They also demonstrated that at the 5-year mark there was a spread of some 30 per cent survival difference in either direction from the 50 per cent average, and that this difference was based purely on psychological state or coping style, i.e., 80 per cent of those with fighting spirit were alive at the 5-year point versus only 20 per cent of the helpless and hopeless. This showed that the 5-year average survival rate normally quoted was completely masking the effect of coping style and that, effectively, the diagnosis of cancer is far more serious for some than for others.

This point has been outlined by the observation that in the USA more women get breast cancer but fewer women die of it than in Britain. Conventional wisdom puts this down to better medical screening and treatment in the States but, given the statistics above, it might equally be that Americans can generally be seen to take a far more assertive, upbeat approach to their diagnosis and illness management.

A great deal of further work in this field through the 1980s and 1990s has come up with the same conclusion: that the state of helplessness and hopelessness and depression in people with cancer is linked to significantly poorer prognosis.[12] Also of great importance is the fact that Dr Greer has gone on to show that people in one of the other more vulnerable categories can be helped to develop a positive coping style if they are given sufficient psychological support.[13] It is therefore absolutely crucial that the positive psychological benefits associated with people becoming involved in fighting their illness, rather than remaining helpless, are recognized and actively encouraged by healthcare professionals and other carers and supporters.

## The effect of support on survival

There is still more evidence that support and emotional expression are crucial to the body's response to disease. This evidence has come from America through the support studies of Dr David Spiegel[2] and Professor Fawzy-Fawzy[3] in the area of cancer medicine, and from Dr Dean Ornish in the field of heart medicine.[14]

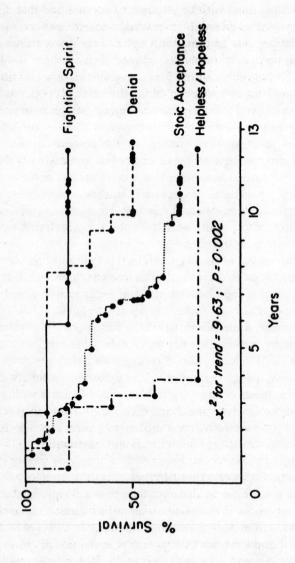

Comparison of survival rates of women with breast cancer who have different coping styles.

Dr Spiegel has shown that expressive psychotherapeutic support given to women with breast cancer for one hour once a week for one year, doubled their survival time over women who did not receive this support. Professor Fawzy-Fawzy showed that giving support to melanoma patients decreased the death rate from 10 per cent in the control group that received no support, to 2 per cent in the group that did receive support; Dr Dean Ornish showed that a programme of psychological support in a group, stress reduction through yoga techniques, exercise, and a low-fat diet, actually reversed coronary artery disease, whilst those that practised diet and exercise alone slowed down the progress of their disease but certainly did not reverse it.

## The effect of visualization on survival

A recent seminal study conducted by Dr Leslie Walker in Scotland has shown that people who used the mind–body techniques of visualization and relaxation during chemotherapy – ostensibly to reduce the side-effects of the chemotherapy – also improved their survival rate.[8] A great number of other studies have also shown the qualitative benefits of relaxation, aromatherapy, meditation and visualization, particularly in symptom control and improvement in quality of life.[15]

# The Link between Nutrition and Cancer

When the Cancer Help Centre opened in 1980 the idea that cancer and nutrition were linked was considered irrational, and the giving of vitamin and mineral supplementation was thought by orthodox doctors to be a waste of time and money. Now, mainstream cancer authorities assert that the poor nutrition associated with Western dietary habits causes 35 per cent cancer mortality in the West.[16] This makes it the highest cause of all (the second highest, at 30 per cent, is smoking). In 1994 Doctors Key and Thorogood reported that having followed 11,000 vegetarians for 17 years they had observed a 25 per cent lower incidence of death from heart disease, 32 per cent lower death rate from strokes, and between 40–50 per cent lower death rate from cancer than in their meat-eating (but otherwise matched) counterparts.[15] There are now several good treatment studies that have all showed that the lives of people with cancer can be extended, and their quality of life improved, by using healthy diet alongside conventional treatments.[16]

With regard to vitamin and mineral supplementation there have been some 10,000 scientific studies looking at the effects of, particularly, the antioxidants C, E, beta-carotene, selenium and zinc on prevention and reversal of cancer. The vast majority of these show very encouraging results, the only concern being that it is inadvisable to take synthetic beta-carotene supplements if you are a smoker as it appears to make things worse rather than better. (Bristol therefore recommends supplements made from naturally occurring beta-carotene.) Most encouraging is an American study conducted in China, which showed that taking the vitamins and minerals A, C, E and selenium reduced the overall death rate from cancer by 13 per cent, and by 20 per cent in their two most common cancers (of the stomach and oesophagus).[17] In the early 1990s, the Bristol Cancer Help Centre compiled a comprehensive database on cancer and nutrition; this is available to those wishing to explore the science further.[5]

The most recent discoveries in the field are showing that it is not just the vitamins and minerals in plant foods that protect us from cancer but also several large families of plant chemicals that are known collectively as phytochemicals. There are many different mechanisms of action involved in this protective effect, but some of these chemicals can actually stabilize and repair DNA and RNA in cell nuclei, repairing and preventing the genetic changes that allow cell lines to become cancerous. This is a staggering discovery because it means that we have to change our image of vegetables as simply being good for our hair and skin to being the absolutely core vital element in protecting and repairing our cells from dangerous genetic mutation. This is no doubt why there have been highly unexpected recoveries in people who put themselves on to rigorous fruit and vegetable fasts and juicing regimes, such as the Gerson diet.

However, to date, we cannot predict which cancers and which individuals will respond to such diets, and further work needs to be done to continue to identify the most potent plant chemicals and their mechanisms of action for cellular repair and protection. Currently the phytochemicals under investigation are indole-glycosinates found in green leafy vegetables and broccoli, phyto-oestrogens found in soya products, phytates, lignans, protease inhibitors, isoflavinoides and isoflavones, which are present in many plant foods and are thought to be inhibitors of oncogenes (the genes that make you predisposed to cancer). Limonene (contained in lemons) and lycopene (in tomatoes) are also anti-cancer phytochemicals, and substances found in shitake mushrooms and the seaweeds kombu and kelp interfere with the initiation and promotion of cancer cells.

Other plant-chemical families under study are plant phenols, aromatic isothyocyonates, methylated flavones, coumarines, and plant sterols, as well as the naturally occurring plant selenium salts, the vitamin C family, with all the accompanying bioflavinoids and cofactors (now thought to be as important as the vitamin itself), and the tocopherols, retinols and carotenes.

In the meantime, it is absolutely clear that high levels of plant material in the diet are quite essential for our health if we are trying to fight or prevent cancer. Carcinogenic contaminants exist in the general environment, and may also be present in the home or work place; they may be created through cooking or food preparation and storage processes, and can gain access to the body via food, air or water. They can also be ingested with tobacco smoke, alcohol and drugs, as well as via radiation and cellular toxins that are accumulated during medical procedures and treatments. Plant phytochemicals materials serve both to protect our cells and to render innocuous any potentially carcinogenic substances ingested into the body.

# The Power of Prayer and Healing

There is random, controlled trial evidence for the power of prayer and spiritual healing in promoting health. It was demonstrated quite clearly that people who were in intensive care units and were prayed for, even without their knowing about it, did significantly better than those who were not.[19] The doctor/healer network has also gone a long way towards collating and publishing existing scientific evidence.[20] Probably the most elegant and convincing research was published in 1998 by the Royal Society of Medicine: GP, Dr Michael Dixon, showed unequivocally that patients receiving healing in his practice, and who had not had relief from conventional medicine in over five years of treatment, had over 50 per cent reduction in their symptoms and distress and equally significant drops in their usage of medication after only ten healing sessions.[22]

3

# *Recovering from Diagnosis and Moving Forward*

Receiving a diagnosis of cancer is probably one of the worst things we can imagine happening to us. Most of us think of it as something that happens to someone else – someone outside our family and circle of close friends. The success of modern medicine creates in us all an expectation that we will live until we are 70 or 80 years old and then die of old age. Most of us feel that good health is our birthright, and that we are basically very strong and well. So the shock of receiving the diagnosis of cancer is absolutely monumental. Nothing prepares us for this disaster: nine times out of ten there will have been hardly any build up or warning that we are about to suffer such a devastating blow.

The effect of shock differs from person to person. But whichever way it is felt or begins to manifest itself the inner turmoil is such that for some time it is almost impossible to hear, and think clearly about, any new information that might be given. This makes an individual acutely vulnerable during this period, and – as at any time in life – it is, wherever possible, important to avoid making any key decisions whilst in shock.

## The Reaction to Diagnosis

For some people, the immediate reaction is highly emotional, whilst for others the first feelings are those of complete numbness. Usually there is a period of intense disbelief and the constant question, 'Why me?', goes round and round in the mind. It seems so random, arbitrary and unfair, and so completely out of context when you may not have felt ill at all. In many cases, putting together a small lump, an odd-looking mole or something that has been detected by routine screening with the information that one's life and future is now critically threatened seems outrageously unbelievable and a total insult to one's sense of 'the way things are'.

For many, this shock becomes quickly coloured by feelings of fear, or even terror, which in the first place may have no definite form, but may then cause physical symptoms such as nausea, diarrhoea, and a racing heartbeat along with terrible panicky feelings of just not knowing how one is going to get through the next five minutes, let alone the whole day. This fear may gradually become more focused, taking the form of more specifically identifiable fears – fear of pain, fear of disfigurement or disability, fear of doctors, hospitals and treatment, and, underlying this in many people's minds, the fear of death itself. Katerina Collins, who had breast cancer, said to me, 'I seriously thought I was going to die of the fear, never mind the cancer. I was even afraid to shut my eyes at night in case I died in my sleep.'

Usually very closely associated with the fear is an intense sense of grief. Often this is felt first in relation to others – children, lovers, parents and friends – because of the unbearable, searing pain at the thought of losing these people. The other major aspect of the grief is the sense of the loss of the future you thought you would have. Usually in this very early stage it can feel almost as though you have died already, as if nothing will ever be the same again. In fact relatives, too, often go into a kind of anticipatory grief. In some cases this can result in prematurely cutting themselves off from the one they love to protect themselves from the insecurity of not knowing whether somebody will live or die, be there for them or not. This feeling that friends and loved ones are withdrawing is acutely painful for the person who is ill, leaving them feeling abandoned with their fear and grief.

For whichever reason – whether it is the distancing by others, being accelerated out of one's everyday state into the contemplation of one's dying, and all the profound spiritual and existential dilemmas this creates, or the intensity of the emotions that are being experienced – the thing that often happens next is a strong feeling of isolation. This can feel like a separation from 'normal' society and 'well' colleagues – as if one has passed through an invisible social barrier to a place from which it is difficult to reach, and be reached, by others who do not understand what is happening to you.

In amongst this can be many complicated feelings towards other people. These can include jealousy that others are living normally, not affected by a threat to their lives, unlike you. It can include resentment and anger about the vulnerable position you are now in, and distrust of others fuelled by the concern about moving from being in control to being dependent or reliant on them, be they family or healthcare professionals. Sometimes this can be associated with a sense of guilt at being a burden or a failure, at ceasing to be the provider or the emotional rock for your friends or family. And, of course, the other side of this will be the great love, closeness and gratitude that you feel as you discover friends and healthcare professionals that you can really trust, and with whom you can allow yourself to be vulnerable and dependent.

There can also be a paradoxical phenomenon happening at the same time: for many, the shock, however awful, can be simultaneously tremendously energizing, triggering a period of heightened clarity and insight. In this state there can be a profound sense of stillness and truth – like being in the eye of the hurricane – so that despite the fact that your life is crashing all around you there can be a very real sense that 'all is well' and that you really do have the inner strength to deal with the ultimate truth of the situation.

## Making the Right Decisions

Of course whilst all this is going on there is a serious imperative to make crucial decisions about the sort of medical help you are going to have. This can be extremely difficult, especially given the complexity and diversity of medical options and protocols available for the treatment of similar cancers, and the vast array of complementary self-help and support options that exist. The confusion and difficulty can be made even greater when health-care professionals are not fully aware of, or trained to deal with, the intense shock reaction you are going through, and this can mean that they try to get you to make key decisions when it is almost impossible for you to think about, and take on board, what is being said.

Part of the problem lies in thinking about and making known your own health beliefs and values. Before making big decisions it is important to be clear about what matters to you in health-care terms, and how you are going to go about dealing with the problem that now faces you. Some cancer healthcare professionals are open to hearing your views and values, but many are not. In the latter case, it will be necessary for you to be even more clear and probably quite assertive in making your values known.

Another issue that strongly affects your ability to make important decisions is the clarity of the picture of your problem you are given. Sometimes cancer healthcare professionals will withhold information on the recommendation of relatives, or will themselves choose to water down what they tell you in order to protect you emotionally. This is quite understandable but can create a false impression. On the other hand, they can make the power of conventional medicine to treat or cure cancer sound stronger than it is. Statistics on the potential of treatments to improve survival may actually reflect only the potential to increase the 'disease-free interval' (the period of time during which you will not be bothered by symptoms or obvious manifestations of the disease). Again it is totally understandable that healthcare professionals should wish to give as upbeat a picture as possible, but clarity is very important if you are to make sound decisions. This question of how completely realistic you wish to be about the 'bottom line' lies very much within your own hands; your doctors and nurses will often be looking for cues from you about how much you wish to know.

## The Medical Reality in Cancer

During this phase of evaluating the conventional medicine on offer there can be a fairly acute sense of disillusionment as we discover the limitations of medicine, and strong feelings of renewed shock that the medical safety net we have taken for granted all our lives may just not be there.

This can be followed by a more chronic sense of growing disillusionment with healthcare professionals themselves who, even if motivated by the desire to help, often try to do so in their terms rather than yours. However, there is a growing trend towards 'patient-centred care', and it is important not to give up in your efforts to communicate your feelings and needs, and to establish good relationships with those that are trying to help you medically – even if you have to teach them how!

## Being Real about How You Feel

The reason for spelling out these reactions in so much detail is that in Britain we tend to feel great embarrassment about our emotions – an abhorrence of losing control, and an inability to allow ourselves to be vulnerable or reliant in any way upon the love, care and efforts of others. This means that we ourselves are often actively suppressing our reaction to the shock, and that others around us – either colleagues, friends, families or health professionals – can also be trying to 'get us back into our box' quickly so that we are not embarrassing, difficult or causing them to feel pain in relation to us.

Often the reaction to the diagnosis can be almost completely swept under the carpet with people being marched straight into rigorous treatments the same day. In the attempt to keep everything as normal as possible, some people do not even stop work whilst undergoing chemotherapy and radiotherapy, and continue to try to maintain their normal social roles within the family and society. This pattern is echoed socially in our collective response to death itself. Frequently the bereaved are given the day off to go to a funeral but apart from that it is 'business as usual', with no space or time whatsoever being given to accommodate the grieving and adjustment process.

At the root of all of this is the fact that as a culture we are not prepared for, or used to, the idea of disease, death and suffering. Most of us tend to live as if we were immortal, repressing and hiding that which is painful or frightening. Whilst it is admirable that the progress of medicine has got us to this point, the way that we fail to integrate the dying process into our lives leaves us extremely vulnerable and unprepared if we are faced with the diagnosis of life-threatening illness in ourselves or in a loved one.

## Taking the Time You Need

Because it is likely that others around you may fail to recognize and make adjustments for the state you are in, it becomes doubly important that you do so. This applies not only at the time of primary diagnosis but if recurrences are diagnosed; then the impact can be even worse than it was the first time around. There can also be points of key vulnerability when your medical treatment stops and you are suddenly left to face the reality of your situation alone, without the care of your medical team and the focus and rigours of your treatment process to occupy centre stage.

In recognizing perhaps just how shocked or upset you are, your primary need will probably be for time – time to take on board what has happened; to feel, express and process your feelings; to think about medical decision-making processes; to get the relevant information you need, and to think about how the diagnosis will affect your life and the lives of those close to you; to think about who you want to tell and how you want to tell them; and time for all the planning for change that diagnosis and treatment will demand. If you are facing treatment, it is very possible that you will need to take leave of absence from work and regular social commitments, and may need to arrange cover for your family and your colleagues. You may well need a good old-fashioned period of convalescence during and after your treatment so that you can recover fully before going back to work, if going back to work at all is appropriate in the bigger picture.

Above all, try very hard to let go of feelings of duty to others during this period. It is very important that you put yourself right at the top of the list of people you look after, and indeed this may be an essential part of what you need to do long-term for your deeper healing process. The period during which you are ill, or in shock, or receiving treatment, is a very good opportunity to get used to doing this.

## Finding the Opportunity within the Crisis

It is a good thing to recognize that, as traumatic and frightening as this time around medical tests and diagnosis is, it is also potentially a very special time in terms of the heightened awareness that it brings. Those learning about the approach of the Bristol Cancer Help Centre have often asked how on earth it can be possible for people to examine their lifestyle and psychological *modus operandi* and make changes in their usual way of being at such an impossibly difficult time. In fact it is almost the only time at which people will make important changes in the behaviours that affect their health and psycho-spiritual well-being.

Anthropologists describe the state induced by the shock of diagnosis as a liminal or threshold state. It is very interesting to note that in many of the early forms of medicine and healing, the process of being taken from one's ordinary state of mind into a liminal state was considered to be the prerequisite for any serious health change or healing to happen, and the process would therefore be deliberately instigated. Examples of this are meditation and breathing techniques, the induction of trance through hypnosis, the whirling, trance-inducing dance in the Sufi healing tradition, or the Native Americans' induction of altered states through the use of psycho-active drugs and sweat-lodges.

One of the key features of the heightened awareness created by the shock of diagnosis is a magnification in your perception of everything that is happening around you. This means that you will feel more acutely whether people are dismissive, distant, cold, authoritarian, or themselves very frightened by what is happening to you, or, conversely, whether they are able to give you proper attention, support, encouragement, love and healing. You will no doubt have found that whilst in this open state negative influences can send you reeling backwards psychologically, whilst supportive, loving and healing environments can cause very positive transformational psychological change. It is therefore important to take time for yourself, or to be with real friends or healers, during this liminal period, not only so that you can protect yourself, and be discriminating about the influences and energies you want around you, but so that you can make the best possible use of this 'transformational window' that is being offered to you.

## Setting Up your Support Network

After recognizing your need for time, the thing you will next need to recognize is your need for support. Most of us are very resistant to the idea of asking for help: we find it embarrassing or humiliating, and we hate the feeling of being 'out of control' or indebted to others. Quite often these feelings are built on our fear of intimacy or on our low self-esteem: we might consider ourselves unworthy of the time and attention of others, feeling that we must pay back anything that is given to us, or we might feel shame at appearing vulnerable emotionally or physically. It is deeply sad that our culture has had this effect on us. The most powerful need in all human beings is for a sense of connection with each other in order that we may give and receive love. Indeed very often, providing the opportunity for others to give is – far from being a burden – a gift for them. Just ask yourself which gives you the better feeling, receiving or giving?

Frequently, though, the problem is that people are not clear enough about the fact that they are in distress and need help – or about the kind of help they do need. Most often, to avoid feelings of dependency and embarrassment, people turn to their very closest person, be that a friend, relative or partner. This is totally natural but has certain inherent problems. First of all your relationship with that person will become dominated by the illness process. Secondly, any existing tensions or weaknesses in the relationship will be exaggerated, potentially critically. Of course the last thing you need is a key relationship crumbling at a time when you are most vulnerable, and certainly the intense needs associated with illness and its treatment are not a particularly good way to try to test, improve or revive a difficult relationship. The third reason is that if most of your distress is being mopped up by the person closest to you, this will almost inevitably in some way, directly or indirectly, rebound on you, in much the same way as a pinball ricochets backwards and forwards within the pinball machine's closed system. In close relationships or family systems the distress, too, ricochets around, affecting first one and then the next member of the family or network, until it comes back to you in perhaps a different form, especially if you are usually the main carer in the family.

It is therefore important to build for yourself a support system that is large enough for the purpose right from the start; this means including sufficient people to spread the load and prevent the support team going into 'support fatigue'. Ideally the team should be made up of those that are sufficiently well supported in their own lives to be able to give what they can give without there being any debt or pay-back needed. It can be good to sit down and, in a very organized way, think of a dozen or so people that you can invite to be part of your support team, asking them explicitly if they can be 'there for you' in one way or another if you need them. This means that when help is essential you already have your support network in place. Having a very real team like this also makes it far less likely that your close carer will sink without trace under the stress and distress they are feeling. In fact if the main support and care is coming from your support team, personal and professional, and your partner, too, finds ways of getting the necessary support and care, there is a genuine chance that the time with your nearest and dearest can be spent in having fun rather than in attempting to counsel and support each other.

Some people have gone so far as to form their support team into a personal support group that meets on a regular basis so that all members of the 'team' of friends can listen to what is going on and hear about what support is needed. This does not have to be a one-way process: it can also be an opportunity for you to listen to what is happening for them, too; and this in itself can be very empowering all round because, as their needs will probably differ from yours, the insight you are gaining through your own process may be of immense value to them. In addition to the friends and loved ones, the support team may well include professional people, such as counsellors, specialist nurses, social workers, ministers, and the team of therapists you find to help you, and it may include members of cancer support groups you meet locally or through the Bristol Cancer Help Centre. Certainly if this issue is addressed head on, and support is organized actively, the difference in facing and planning for what has to be faced on a day-to-day basis is enormous.

An excellent example of how this can work is the story of Veronica Mills, who came to the Centre in the early 1980s. She had gone to have a mole removed from her chin for cosmetic reasons when it was discovered that the mole was a melanoma. She was told that there was serious metastases in her liver and that she had only three months to live. She was utterly determined that this would not be the case, especially since she had only recently adopted two children. In fact, she lived for over nine years from the time of her diagnosis – until both children were out of school. Very early on in the weeks that followed her diagnosis she realized that nearly all of her friends had stopped telephoning her, and she sensed that they were completely at a loss as to what to say or how to help. Amazingly she wrote a 'round robin letter' to everyone she knew saying:

Dear Friend,
Yes, I have cancer. Yes, I have been told I have only three months left to live – but actually I am still here! And I need:

1.  Flowers every week.
2.  Somebody to pick up my organic vegetables each week.
3.  Money for my holistic therapy.
4.  Somebody to take my children out while I meditate and visualize.
5.  A holiday in the Bahamas.
6.  Any information any of you can find about alternative treatment for cancer anywhere in the world ...

And her list went on and on, detailing about 20 practical ways in which people could help her. Veronica got absolutely every single thing on her list – and more – along with letters of intense gratitude from the people who loved her saying, 'Thank God you told us what we could do to help. We were aching to do something but didn't have a clue what would make a difference.'

Veronica's approach was exceptionally up front, but it beautifully illustrates the point that for most of us there is probably a great deal more help available within our social network than we would ever imagine if only we can become clear about what it is that we need, and then let go of our inhibitions and ask for it. All we have to do is be prepared for the answer No if some-body recognizes that at this point they are not in a position to help – and that is quite all right too.

If you do not have strong social networks it is all the more important to get yourself to cancer support groups or local community groups like your church, a yoga class, or anywhere where kind, loving people meet, and make your need known. One of the loveliest things that people have said about Bristol over the years is, 'We could not believe the incredible amount of love we received from total strangers.' This emphasizes even more strongly the point that, sometimes, stepping out of one's family and social network can open up the possibility of receiving help from sources you never even imagined were there, and indeed enriching the lives of others by giving them the opportunity to be helpful and to express their care.

Along with finding sources of support, get really practical and, like Veronica, make a list of absolutely everything you need. Then begin asking – either directly or by letter – for the items on the list. Having your list worked out also means that when friends spontaneously offer help, you do not waste the golden opportunity: you will be prepared and will know exactly what to ask for. You will find very quickly that with a little bit of practice the embarrassment goes and it starts to feel quite natural. Whilst you're at it, ask your family what they need. In this way you can short-circuit the problem of growing resentment as they begin to see the things you have asked for flowing towards you!

## Getting the Information You Need, and Making the Right Choices

Because of the intensity of the initial reaction to the diagnosis of cancer, and the inadequacy of the social and medical help that individuals are given during the early intense period of vulnerability, two reactions are common. Some people collapse and give up altogether, turning their faces to the wall, living on in a state of great fear and intimidation, while others attempt to submerge their feelings altogether, going into a kind of denial and trying as quickly as possible to get life 'back to normal'. Both of these responses are completely understandable, but it is far better if support can be found to face and express the feelings, for this will make it much easier to begin the process of starting to take control of your situation. The process of taking control usually starts with gathering information and seeing what choices you have in terms of how you tackle your cancer and the emotional upheaval it has caused.

The information you will need falls into four main categories:

1. Medical information about your condition and its treatment.

2. Information about complementary, alternative and self-help approaches.

3. Information about support services.

4. Practical information about how the cancer services operate in your area.

(You will find some relevant telephone numbers and contact addresses relating to this section in Appendix II.)

## 1. Medical information

The best agency in Britain dealing with medical information about cancer and its treatment is CancerBACUP (formerly BACUP, British Association of Cancer Unit Patients). Cancer-BACUP have an extensive range of leaflets about all types of cancer and its treatment, and a telephone helpline to answer more specific questions. This can be very useful if you find your own medical team have not given you enough time to ask all the questions you need to ask. It can also be a lot less daunting than medical libraries, where information is written up in very stark terminology, which can be alienating and frightening because it has been written for those treating, rather than experiencing, cancer.

What you will probably not get from CancerBACUP is information about pioneer techniques or experimental clinical trials, which may be happening at the cutting edge of medicine. It can be very useful to try to track down who is leading the field in your particular kind of cancer. This can usually be discovered by talking to medical personnel in your oncology centre, or by phoning the colleges of the particular disciplines involved. The other source of this information is the Cancer Research Campaign or the Imperial Cancer Research Fund, or indeed the Institute of Cancer Research through which much of the research work is actually carried out.

Having gathered this information you may then wish to compare it with what is going on in America. Here the first step may be to contact the American Cancer Society, who will be able to point you towards leaders in the field in America. Alternatively the Sloane Kettering Memorial Hospital is another good source of information about American advances. All of these organizations will have (usually very helpful) information departments. There is of course also the Internet, but the problem here is dealing with the huge quantity and complexity of the information that you are likely to find. Nevertheless it may be a good starting place so that you can cross-reference the information you are getting from the various sources, and begin to see which way the path is leading.

It is important to find out from the hospital cancer service, your GP, health visitors, and the nursing support services, exactly what facilities and services there are available to you through the NHS and voluntary sectors both locally and throughout the country. People with cancer often complain that they only discovered much later about valuable local services that they would have used if they'd known about them. There may also be many practical ways you could be receiving help, financially, socially and emotionally. Many cancer centres and units are in the process of building good information units, and you may be lucky and find that your own treatment centre has both the information and somebody there who can lead you through it.

Once you have gathered the information you need, you may wish to return to discuss it with your consultant or to seek a second opinion with whoever it is you have discovered is leading the field in the speciality that relates to you (*see* box). Another possibility is to seek a consultation with an holistic doctor who will be able to give you help in exploring the different options and asking the right questions when you meet the doctors involved (*see* page 121).

---

### Seeking a second opinion

Currently, everybody is entitled to a second opinion on the NHS. If you discover that there are better treatments for your condition in parts of the country other than in your own health authority area, you are entitled to an extra contractual referral (ECR) to enable you to take advantage of them. However, in practice, this means that the degree of success that you have in obtaining help from elsewhere often reflects the amount of detective work you are prepared to put in, and the assertiveness with which you pursue other avenues of help. Whilst it is unacceptable that there should be such a degree of demographical variation in standards and knowledge available, it is the reality of the situation, and we are therefore obliged to take account of it.

---

## 2. *Complementary, alternative and self-help approaches*

It is hoped that your need for information about the holistic approach to cancer will have been met by reading this book or watching the Bristol Cancer Help Centre's introductory video 'The Holistic Approach To Health'. In either case it will be abundantly clear that it is necessary to address the psycho-spiritual components of your illness as well as the physical.

In addition to the holistic approach described here, there are many more physically orientated alternative therapies for the treatment of cancer. The best book currently available on this subject is *The Definitive Guide To Cancer*, by W. John Diamond, W. Lee Cowden and Burton Goldberg (*see* Further Reading). The book details the protocols of 37 alternative cancer doctors and all the different medicines they use to tackle the cancer and boost the body's abilities to heal itself.

You can also investigate the various options by exploring the alternative cancer treatment websites. Many of the alternative clinics (*see* Appendix II) will happily send you information about their protocols and the treatments they use, or will make staff available to talk to you about what is on offer.

Again, once you have collected the information you need you may be somewhat overwhelmed by the diversity of what you have discovered. It may be wise to seek an appointment with an holistic doctor who can help you to consider all the options and work out which one is the most suitable for you. Bear in mind, though, that not all alternative medical treatments take into account the underlying state of spirit and mind which is crucial to immune functioning in the longer term. It may therefore be necessary for you to organize the mind–body aspect of your approach in addition to any alternative treatment you decide to use as part of your overall plan.

Once you have sifted through the information and made informed choices, you can embark on the treatments you have chosen in the empowering knowledge that the medical help you are receiving is one part of a much bigger picture that you now see clearly. You will, it is hoped, have taken on board that you can be as powerful an agent in your own defence as the medical treatment that is being offered to you, and that even if there is no medical treatment on offer there are many very significant steps you can take to increase the possibility of living with cancer.

The Bristol Approach is unique in Britain, and almost unique in the world, in offering in-depth mind–body medicine. The approach dramatically improves the ability to cope with the diagnosis and treatment of cancer, improves the chances of survival, and ultimately can turn the crisis of cancer into the opportunity for living far more happily and healthily than before. (There are three other significant holistic centres in the world: in California, Melbourne and Tel Aviv. *See* Appendix II.) The Bristol Approach has a great deal to offer anyone, but it is especially important for those who feel that their spirit has been crushed by difficult and painful life events, or who have lost their way in life, or who recognize themselves as self-stressors or workaholics, or who are aware that their energy levels or mood are low, or that in one way or another they do not take very good care of their health.

Not all aspects of the Bristol Approach will be right for everyone, but usually the obvious starting point will become clear quickly, and it may be that over time your use of the approach will increase as you explore it further – a bit like peeling the different layers from an onion. For example, over four years in her recovery from the treatment for secondary ovarian cancer, Sarah Hughes of Bristol tackled first her nutrition and physical health. In year two she moved, having initially resisted it, into counselling, unburdening herself of the considerable emotional distress she was carrying; in year three she used energy medicines, which significantly enhanced her level of health, and, in year four, she was able to embrace her spirituality by joining the Quakers and thus finally to put the whole jigsaw together.

Many have said how they wished that healing could be a nice straightforward affair, after which one could carry on life as before. But, in the immortal words of Penny Brohn, 'healing is a process, not an event', and the different parts of the healing process go on at different levels at different rates. It is therefore important to remain open to this healing process even when you feel inclined to close the book and try not to think about it. At times, the way forward will be clear, but at others it will be obscure. This is why it is wise to organize as much support as possible, so that you can draw on it when you lose the plot and need help, encouragement and guidance.

## 3. Support services

Britain has a number of support groups and centres that have been developed by people who have used the Bristol Approach (*see* Appendix II). These groups are absolutely ideal for people who will use the Bristol Approach as they will get support in finding the right kind of therapists, learning the self-help techniques, and maintaining a strong positive attitude. There are in excess of 600 further support groups around Britain, which are held in a directory by Cancerlink. In addition to these there are disease- and problem-specific support groups, which should be known to your cancer centre/unit information service or to Cancerlink.

Other kinds of support agencies include those that deal with legal, financial, social and nursing care needs. Again these should be known to your cancer unit/centre but, if not, send for the Bristol Cancer Help Centre's National Organization List or Macmillan Cancer Relief's 'Help is There' leaflet. (*See* Appendix II.)

## 4. Your local cancer services

It may serve you very well at difficult moments to know exactly how the cancer services operate in your area, so it is worth finding out all you can as soon as possible. For example, you may wish to know the management structure and overall policy for your area. You may wish to find out what facilities and practical help there is available, what support and complementary services are provided, and indeed what the attitude is regarding these services in your area. You may want to know how to access the help of specialist nurses – Macmillan, Marie-Curie or the local community nurse, for example – and what role your GP will play. You may wish to visit your local hospice, or know how to access specialist pain control or get second opinions. You may wish to know if your GP is allowed to prescribe you vitamins, or if your area health authority provides complementary therapies routinely, or will pay for alternative treatment if you conventional treatment is no longer working.

Some of this information will be available from the information centre at the hospital where you are being treated. Some will be available from the GP, or local primary care group committee, and some from the local headquarters of the nursing services. If you are nor getting the answers you need, or feel concerned about what you are discovering, you should contact the director or manager of cancer services for your area through your local cancer centre/unit or health authority.

# PART TWO

# GETTING YOURSELF GOING

# 4

# *Working with Holistic Therapies*

Whether it is through embarking upon the Bristol Approach, or by making your own assessment of your state and needs, it is important to determine your therapeutic priorities and to decide which therapies you will use. You will then need to know how to go about finding the best therapists in your area to give you the help you need. There are two levels on which your therapeutic priorities can be assessed:

1. In relation to the promotion of your overall health in order to fight your cancer.

2. In relation to the symptoms of cancer and side-effects of treatment.

These two points – or levels of assessment – are interrelated in that the improvement of one's overall health is an important factor in reducing the severity of symptoms. Having said this, there are many useful holistic interventions that target specific symptoms, and these are dealt with fully in Chapter 8. In this chapter, we shall concentrate on the primary factors that affect your overall health, and the ways in which you can begin to control them. There are seven main areas that you will need to look at and assess:

These are your:

1. Spiritual state.
2. Energy levels.
3. Emotional and mental state.
4. Physical state.
5. Environment.
6. Lifestyle.
7. Relationships.

## Spiritual State

The most important factor is the state of your spirit. To assess your spiritual state, you will need to begin by asking yourself two vital questions:

- Do I really have the will to live?
- Does my life still have a purpose and meaning that is genuinely to do with me and my own self-expression (rather than with being here purely for others, be they children, elderly parents or partner)?

Whilst the other people in your life are vital considerations it is really important to look at how your unique life energy is expressed. The other side of this question is whether or not you have sources of uplift and nourishment for your spirit, and whether you take the time to build these into your life. Behind all of this is the question of whether you feel fundamentally connected to life and society or whether you have come to feel isolated and separate.

If you recognize that your spirit is crushed, or that you feel disillusioned or lost in life, it would be extremely beneficial to get involved either in the Bristol programme or in transpersonal psychotherapy to literally 'bring yourself back to life'. It may also be important to have spiritual healing regularly to lift your spirit.

# Energy Levels

At the beginning of any holistic health programme – and indeed from then onwards on a day-to-day basis – it is extremely important to ask yourself what is going on with your energy. (*See also* Chapter 2.) To begin with you need to try to 'tune in' to what is happening to your energy, and this is easiest to do after a relaxation exercise. Often people will say, 'My energy levels are great – I can keep going for hours and hours,' but the minute they relax and let go they discover that they are too exhausted to stay awake. This phenomenon occurs when people override the body's signals of exhaustion by 'pumping themselves up', often with the aid of coffee, cigarettes, and other stimulants, in order to induce the feeling of 'high energy' whilst actually running on empty. It is continuing to work hard for prolonged periods in this kind of state that often results in 'burn-out' or the 'TATT (tired all the time) syndrome'; burn-out occurs when the override mechanism finally breaks down and the individual is forced to acknowledge the depth of their tiredness.

The next step has two parts. First you must analyse where or how you are expending all your energy, and whether it is in ways that really profit you or that leave you unsatisfied, resentful or even feeling abused. Then you must identify the things that refresh you and genuinely give you energy. Once you have made these distinctions, you can begin to replace the former with the latter. As you become better at staying in touch with your energy, you can get down to finer and finer tuning as you begin to ask yourself, 'Do I really wish to put my energy into that phone call, that shopping trip into the centre of town, organizing that event, propping up that draining relationship? Or do I wish to let these things go so that I can conserve and build my energy and enjoy using it?'

You may also begin to notice how much of your energy is wasted through accumulation of physical tension in the body, or by 'over-egging the pudding' socially or professionally. Do you put twice as much energy into everything as you really need to, and feel resentful when others don't notice or don't appreciate all the effort you have made?

If, when making your initial assessment of your energy state, you realize that your energy levels are very low then it is important to pull back immediately from your normal commitments and to start seeing a healer or a practitioner of either acupuncture, shiatsu or homoeopathy so that you can begin to build your vital energy again quickly.

## Emotional and Mental State

You will need to assess your emotional and mental state both in terms of your reaction to diagnosis and treatment of cancer, and in terms of the state that predominated prior to diagnosis.

In the section on recognizing your state and needs in Chapter 3, I have gone into great detail about the effects of the shock of diagnosis. It is very likely that in the short term you will need a counsellor to help you express the distress you are feeling, grieve for the losses you are experiencing, and gradually enable you to get your feet back on the ground somewhat adjusted to the reality of the situation you are now facing. Some people prefer to do this in a support group with others going through the same experience. It can be extremely helpful to meet other people that are living with their cancer because they will understand exactly how you feel.

Whilst your tendency may be to 'batten down the hatches' or 'get a grip', it is far better for you to try to let go at this point and 'feel' your feelings. Otherwise the body becomes a bit like a pressure cooker, full of unexpressed emotion, and this is not a good state to be in long term, especially if you are undergoing any treatment.

As part of the bigger picture you may want to start asking yourself whether you have been involved in any severe emotional trauma in the two to three years preceding the onset of your cancer, and whether you feel that you have been harbouring a lot of pain, grief, anger or fear, or perhaps feelings of hurt, rejection or resentment. Behind all of this is the question, How do you deal with your emotions generally? Are you able to express your feelings as they arise? Or do you censor everything, pushing down what you feel so that you don't embarrass yourself or others, or risk others' disapproval?

Another thing to look at is the way your mind works. You may recognize yourself as being extremely 'stuck in your head'. This in itself can be a symptom of stress, or of feeling frightened or threatened, because as explained previously the very first step of the physiological stress response is to prioritize thinking and muscular functions. It may, on the other hand, mean that you are more of an intellectual than a feeling type. Or you may be somebody whose mind is constantly working, churning over all the options and possibilities, and stressing yourself quite severely in the process.

At this point you may also start to identify the 'drivers' or motivational factors underlying most of your behaviour. Are these driving forces based on fear – of loneliness, rejection, destitution, violence, or of dying – and is this previous motivational axis of your life appropriate to your current situation? For example the memories of a violent childhood may mean that we are living our lives in a very fearful state, and continuing to expend a great deal of energy in the avoidance of conflict and disharmony because as a little child the violence was perceived to be literally a threat to our lives. In adult life, whilst confrontation may be unpleasant it is not necessarily life-threatening, and a combination of an individual's fear levels and the effort they are putting into 'being nice' or 'striving for harmony' may be exhausting them and making it difficult to sustain solid, intimate relationships. It is very possible that you may be able to use this time of heightened intensity – of being in the 'liminal state' described earlier (*see* pages 55–6) – to choose to abandon these strategies or ways of being, and reorientate yourself around new motivations and core values associated with your personal fulfilment and creative self-expression.

Within the field of cancer medicine, and the support services that surround it, there is increasing provision for helping the initial distress, either through access to specialist nurse counsellors, or through counselling provided routinely by your oncology unit or GP's practice. This is quite different from the counselling pioneered at Bristol, which enables people with cancer and their supporters to look very deeply at how their normal state of mind and emotional reality is affecting their body's ability to resist or recover from disease.

If any of these issues are relevant to you then the Bristol programme will be highly appropriate, as will finding a transpersonal counsellor in your own area to continue the counselling process locally (or to initiate such counselling if you are unable to come to Bristol). Unlike psychoanalysis, transpersonal counselling is not usually a long process. You may find that your psychological re-orientation occurs within only weeks of having regular sessions.

## Physical State

When starting to assess your physical state the main questions you will need to ask yourself are:

- How do I eat?
- What is my body's state of fitness?
- How do I hold myself posturally, and what are my breathing patterns like?'
- How well do I express my physicality in dance and sport?
- Do I express my sexuality in a satisfying way?

### Diet
If your eating is far from healthy you may need the help of a nutritional therapist to guide you into a healthy eating pattern and to give you the emotional support necessary to make the changes.

Changing the way we eat can be difficult, especially if there are other stresses going on. It is very important to do it in a way that will minimize the risk of failure, and a nutritional therapist will help you do this. *Healing Foods Cookbook*, the wholefood cookery book by Jane Sen, the Bristol Centre's catering consultant, is also helpful; Appendix I contains some sample recipes.

## Exercise and physical expression

All of us require exercise. We should take at least 20 minutes of aerobic exercise twice a week. But, just as important, we all need to stretch (as cats and dogs demonstrate so beautifully). Many of us have very sedentary lifestyles, spending hours in front of desks, driving cars or sitting in front of TVs or computers. It is extremely important to stretch our spines, joints, muscles, ligaments and tendons; this has the effect of 'massaging' our internal organs, which ensures that the blood-flow to all areas of the body remains good; this in turn helps to prevent the build-up of toxicity or calcium deposits in the tissues, which are places where cancer tends to develop. So, whatever happens, a basic stretch and breathe routine, such as the one taught on the Bristol therapy programme, will serve you very well in your recovery process. It would also be extremely helpful to seek out local yoga, t'ai chi or chi gong classes.

On the other hand, you may be the sort of person for whom physical expression is an extremely important part of your creativity, but have abandoned this part of yourself as the pressures of parenthood or work mounted, or as inertia took over. If you know deep down that your body aches to dance, jump, climb, hand-glide, skate or run, then it is extremely important that you should respond to this and start doing it (though you should of course break yourself in again gently). Cancer rates are considerably lower in people who exercise, and it may be very significant that Penny Brohn, who lived for 20 years with breast cancer and its bony recurrences, swam 50 lengths three times a week until very near the end of her life.

## Sexuality

It may be important to ask how your sexual energy is manifesting itself, as unexpressed sexual energy may make us bad tempered or violent, obsessive or driven.

---

### Rechannelling sexual energy

The issue of how to express our sexuality fully is a complex one because much depends on our compatibility with – or indeed the presence of – a partner. If, for whatever reason, we feel 'stuck' or limited in our sexuality, help is available either conventionally, from sex therapists, or through Tantra training. Tantra is a form of yoga in which one learns how to channel sexual energy into the higher energy centres or *chakras* in the body in order to open ourselves to higher states of consciousness, and it can be very helpful as it provides an alternative, but satisfactory and fun, way of expressing this energy.

The Tantra training offered in Britain currently focuses on what it is that gets in the way of our pleasure and enjoyment of our sexuality, and how we can heal the shame, inhibition, fear and abusive elements of our sexuality. This fits in very well with the holistic approach. Both couples and single people can undertake and benefit from Tantra training.

---

## Environmental Influence

Health problems can be caused by environmental stresses, either social or physical. For example, many people have helped themselves to become well by removing themselves from the influence of a very overpowering personal relationship – 'taking back their power' and re-establishing their autonomy. Similarly, people have become well again after recognizing that the building, or even the city, in which they live or work, makes them feel unwell. Your home environment can be checked for what is called geopathic stress (*see* Appendix II); this is done by dowsers or physicists, who look for high and low areas of magnetic, electro-magnetic or radio-active energy, which can markedly affect health.

The main thing is to trust your intuition. If you quieten down and ask yourself how your living and working environment is making you feel you may well be surprised to discover how much you already know and the extent to which you have been ignoring your own 'inner knowing.'

## Lifestyle

Your lifestyle will reflect the state of your spirit, emotions and mind, and vice versa. Ask yourself the questions:

- Is my lifestyle in balance?
- Am I balancing my work with leisure activities, my times of busyness with stillness?
- Do I take time purely for myself, without planned activity, to be reflective and develop creativity?

If, in answering these questions, you can see that your lifestyle is out of balance and that your quality of living has become severely reduced it can be useful, with the help of an holistic doctor or counsellor, to address this problem head on and decide how you are going to make the appropriate changes.

This will inevitably mean some letting go. Many of us are workaholic or perfectionist, or perhaps just plain greedy in terms of the amount we take on. We can't bear to abandon our projects or hand them over to others with whom they may fail or, worse still, do better than when we were at the helm! Some of us are so bad at controlling our work that we allow it to leak into and take over all areas of our life; in such cases we need to schedule time with ourselves and our families, or put our new creative or self-help activity into the diary in the same way we would timetable work appointments. This can be a good trick in establishing a new lifestyle – entering these times into the diary a long way ahead, and fitting work activity around them as opposed to the other way around.

Some of us require a physical symbol of making this space in our lives for ourselves. This might take the form of a room of our own, or even an area in an existing room in the house, where we can be 'in our own space', surrounded by what is significant to us. Usually it is people whose lives are the most caught up in the needs of others who most strongly need to take this action.

## Your Relationships

### *Your relationship with yourself and others*

Almost everything that has been mentioned so far is about developing a new relationship with yourself. The very process of asking yourself questions and evaluating your state means that you have begun to take notice of how you are and how the things around you affect you. It is important to think clearly about what time, attention and care you give yourself, and what this says about your relationship with yourself. Ask yourself whether you think you are actually abusive towards yourself. For instance:

- Do I harm myself with cigarettes or excessive alcohol or drugs?
- Do I set myself crazy targets or actually harm myself physically?
- Do I stay in relationships in which I am being hurt or mistreated?

You may be prone to chronically abandoning yourself, i.e., putting everybody else's needs before your own. Further, you may despise yourself for getting caught up in sado-masochistic relationships with yourself and others, and this can initiate and maintain a cycle of self others and allowing yourself to be abused. These cyclical patterns can take myriad different forms and involve any number of different people – parents, colleagues, lovers and friends – but whatever the context the effect is to leave you feeling alienated and unnourished.

The dynamics of our relationship with ourselves will determine how much love we are able to let in, how much help we will allow ourselves to receive, and whether we will be able to build a new life that is balanced, wholesome and healthy, and truly reflects who we are.

Honesty with ourselves is the key to finding out what we need to do. If we know that in our relationships with others we have been habitually rather dominant, overpowering and selfish, we may need to learn how to soften, to listen, and to serve the needs of others. If our pattern has been to abandon ourselves and allow ourselves to be dominated, we shall need to learn how to know and express our needs, and to become more assertive.

The success we have in breaking these cycles will ultimately depend on whether we can bear to be on our own until a new, healthier relationship develops. This in turn depends on our developing a new relationship with ourselves: as we become less needy and dependent, we compromise ourselves less and become more self-sufficient. There are many ways we can develop a better relationship with ourselves and others, either through help from a skilled counsellor or through developmental group work.

## Your relationship with life and the divine

Ask yourself the following questions:

- Do I feel supported by life or do I feel like an island, permanently cut off and battling for survival?
- Do I believe in the possibility that there is a planetary life-

force or higher, intelligent, loving consciousness that can assist me? Or,

- Do I feel entirely separate and alone in the world?'

Two of the most powerful experiences people have in embracing the holistic approach are first, the discovery of their own personal power, which becomes apparent as they begin to develop both their sense of purpose and their creative will through visualization and affirmation processes, and, second, the discovery of how much loving help there is within the universe if they only become receptive to it and ask for it.

To make the first discovery involves moving out of a passive relationship with life and beginning, through the process of visualization and affirmation, to start choosing the way you want things to be. This can be done in images or in words, and is remarkably powerful. Practising visualization brings one up against one's 'limiting beliefs', which are the voices that tell us we can't possibly be successful or have things the way we want them. Given sufficient encouragement and support, however, these barriers can be traversed with very exciting results. But equally exciting is the diametrically opposite process, which is learning to 'let go and let God'. For people who constantly take control in all situations this moment may be reached only in extremis. For others, beginning the process of 'handing over to a higher power' comes more easily.

Just as taking control of your own life sets free a whole set of forces that can then come to your assistance, so letting go and surrendering to God or the universe, and asking for the appropriate help, can set in motion another set of processes that allows all manner of unforeseen help to come to your assistance and to the assistance of those around you. Formal help is available to assist you in initiating these processes, but both are much simpler than you may imagine at first.

In my opinion these two processes form a paradoxical but highly effective blueprint for living for all of us – directing us towards being able to move back and forth between our active, creative, individuated self, and our surrendered, expanded sense of self where we give up our sense of control, and hand over our trust to the life process. In establishing this level of flexibility we can develop a very strong sense of self whilst simultaneously learning to let go and 'go with the flow' of life, even if ultimately this means flowing into our dying. As one spiritual teacher said, 'We must learn how to take hold tightly and let go lightly.'

## Therapeutic Priorities

Reading through this section on the holistic appraisal will have given you an idea of what is going through the minds of holistic doctors, counsellors, healers, nurses and therapists as they take you through the therapeutic assessment processes. Once your needs are established, you and your therapy team can determine your therapeutic priorities. These may include help in facing the cancer diagnosis, making treatment decisions, facing and going through cancer treatments and dealing with the symptoms of your illness, and the much bigger process of setting about promoting your health 'from the inside out'.

Your therapeutic priorities will change over time as healing begins to take place, and this is why regular reassessment and review is important. The ideal situation is to have an holistic doctor as an anchor point to which you can refer from time to time, and your own team of counsellor, healer and energy therapist whom you see on a regular basis in your home area.

You may decide that your first priority is to take an alternative medical/metabolic route by visiting one of the treatment centres in Europe or America. You may also wish to see a Chinese or a European herbalist for help in treating your cancer. If this is what you want to do, it is still extremely helpful to have an assessment with an holistic doctor first. You can then get a sense of how serious your cancer is and whether you may be best advised to take at least some medical help to avert any immediate danger.

## Facing the Fears

An extremely important part of the holistic approach is learning to look absolutely head on at the things that are scaring you. Of course you need the right level of support and 'holding' in order to do this. This may come from an individual counsellor or from a group. It is quite remarkable how much better you will feel if you can allow yourself to name and explore your fears.

When you begin to do this, you will quite probably discover that the thing that is really worrying you is not quite what you thought it was. For example, people who say they are terrified of operations quite often find that it is not the operation itself that scares them but rather the implicit loss of control. When they find out exactly what it is that is bothering them it makes it possible to start doing something about it – conveying this fear to healthcare professionals; asking them to give you as much information as humanly possible about what is going to happen and how you will get help if you need it; what procedures, tubes and stitches you will have; how you will get pain relief; whether you can give the final go ahead to the anaesthetist when you feel ready, and so on.

Similarly, when people examine their fear of dying, they often discover that it is not so much dying itself that frightens them but rather the question of how they will die: whether they will suffer, whether they will be 'a nuisance to others', or whether the process will involve their becoming disabled and dependent – losing control – and having to allow others, who don't know them that well, to take over at such a significant time – a time when they feel at their most vulnerable. Often the greatest fear of all is the pain of letting go of relatives and loved ones. But in 'speaking the unspeakable', and by grieving and 'finishing the emotional business' with others, there can be immense relief. And in being helped to think about, or even plan, your dying process – however far in the future it may be – and talking about this to your closest carers, you can also be relieved of a great deal of worry and stress.

Once you have tackled these really big fears – and realized how much better you feel when you can look at and communicate what is going on inside – you may find that you get a taste for it. This means that you can look at what is frightening you regularly, first with your counsellor but later perhaps with others with whom you have personal relationships. You can take turns with your loved ones to say what you are feeling, and then what you need. For the other person, the object is not to intervene or necessarily even say anything; instead it is to provide a supportive listening presence, while resisting the urge to find solutions or 'make you feel better'. And rather than expect that person to jump in and try to fulfil a need, the object of expressing your feelings is to bring them to full consciousness, which not only makes you feel better but means that you have a much clearer map of what is going on for you. Quite often you will find that the process of articulating these things changes them, and begins to alter the way you feel, liberating you to move on through and out of the other side of this dark forest of fears.

## Learning to Care for Yourself

If you have never really thought much about yourself or your needs perhaps the biggest challenge of all when adopting the holistic approach is this learning to care for yourself. I can remember one visitor to the Cancer Help Centre recalling a comment made by one of her therapists at home: 'Think carefully about getting involved with the holistic approach – it will involve your committing yourself, your time and your money to the process.' The person involved had at first recoiled, thinking, 'I can't possibly do that – spend money on, and take time for, myself – how selfish'. But as the days went on, she gradually realized that investing in herself is the essence of the holistic recovery process.

## Caring for yourself – the essential ingredients

- Think about getting it right for yourself in all situations. Whilst this may initially feel selfish and uncomfortable – like crossing your arms the wrong way – you will quickly find that if you learn to get things right for you it will be far better for everybody else around you.

- Take time for yourself. Allocate several days and evenings a month which are solely your time. Make this unstructured time that you can use as appropriate when it arrives. Use these times to be reflective, and to do only things that soothe, nurture and lift your spirit. In addition to this, make regular time for your important therapeutic sessions or self-help classes.

- Be gentle with yourself. Do not make the holistic approach another stick with which to beat your back. There are absolutely no shoulds or oughts involved in any of the many aspects of the holistic approach. It is not about setting yourself gigantic tasks, feeling guilty if you fail, and in general feeling too great a responsibility for yourself and your health. Quite the reverse: it is about identifying the aspects of yourself that tend to push you too hard, and allowing yourself to find a new way of being – one that is gentle, spontaneous and feels very right to you. Remember you are the only one who can judge that.

- Prioritize activities that excite and enthuse you, and allow you self-expression.

- Let go of your concerns about the opinions of others.

- Most important of all, be yourself.

In order to help people become accustomed to the idea of forging this new relationship with themselves, I suggest that they think of themselves as a child in their own care. If this child was ill they would make absolutely sure the child went to bed early, had lots of treats and words of encouragement, and had the best food; if the child had no appetite, they would sit with them at mealtimes and try all manner of means to tempt them to eat.

Some people find that establishing this new relationship with the self can seem quite daunting, and they find it difficult to know where to start. In such cases it helps to begin the process gradually: make a few simple changes that are sustainable, and then begin to take further steps towards bigger changes as the needs become apparent. Other people see absolutely clearly the changes they need to make from early on in their process, and they may be able to make dramatic changes in one fell swoop. In all cases, the healing journey is intensely personal, and should be undertaken at your own pace. It is very important not to judge yourself or compare yourself with others who may appear to be doing more than you. Often the inner changes people make can have more profound effects than the dramatic-looking external life changes.

## Making Progress

You will soon find that having regular therapeutic input from your healer, counsellor and energy therapist will make a very big difference to your state and ability to cope. In fact, after doing the introductory days and residential week at Bristol, and/or having several counselling sessions at home with a transpersonal therapist, you may start to glimpse the potential that is involved in this crisis.

As I have said earlier, working with the holistic approach can be compared to renovating a garden. Think of yourself as both garden and gardener, and set about the renovation process in stages:

1. First remove anything that is choking your life-force: this might be over-activity, difficult interpersonal situations, self-stressing attitudes, and so on.

2. In the second phase, look to see where in the garden the new life is emerging, and encourage this growth; this is the phase of therapy when you spend time focusing on what is right about you, reminding yourself of what gives you pleasure and really makes your heart sing, and receiving the encouragement and support you need to blossom in your true colours.

3. In the third phase we must look again at the garden to see whether there are any earthworks that need to be done, i.e., putting in a new feature or moving existing plants to more appropriate places. In therapy, this is the time when you may want to look at some of the deeper issues that have been thwarting your potential and progress in life. It may also be the time when you want to contemplate making bigger life changes, such as changing your job or moving house, or perhaps sorting out a difficult, dysfunctional relationship.

The point of reminding you of this staged approach is that it is important to be wise about the timing and pace of any changes you make: you need to take into account the state of your physical health and the strength of the foundations you have laid inside yourself through your earlier therapy to ensure that a particular change is a good one.

It is important to ensure that change is being made for the right reasons, and that you are not merely running away from some aspect of yourself. In Alcoholics Anonymous meetings, they call this 'doing a geographical', which means thinking that a problem can be solved by moving away from it physically rather than by tackling it on the psychological level. Whilst physical moves may be required in the long term (as can be seen in stage 3 of our garden analogy) it is usually better to start with the work of sorting out the ways you are stressing or distressing yourself first – by working through stages 1 and 2 – otherwise you are likely to take these problems with you wherever you go.

A time will come when you realize you have reached a new level of stability and health, and at this stage it begins to feel possible to embark upon the regular practice of self-help. At this point the need for your therapy sessions begins to diminish. Your therapists will help to guide you in deciding when it is an appropriate time to stop therapy. Energy therapists in acupuncture

---

### Choosing a therapist

It can be difficult to know how to set about choosing the right holistic therapist for you or finding the relevant classes or support agencies locally or nationally.

A comprehensive list of parent body organizations of the different therapeutic and self-help specialities are given in Appendix II; they can tell you of well-qualified practitioners in your area, and the other voluntary agencies listed can give you specific information about your cancer, its treatment, and the support groups around you.

When you talk to the parent bodies of the therapeutic organizations, it is helpful to mention that you have cancer and that you want an experienced practitioner who is confident to work with people with cancer. It is also a good idea to say that you are working with the Bristol Approach.

If you are struggling it may be best to phone the Bristol Cancer Help Centre helpline for further advice. The team at the Centre have over the years built up many high-quality therapist contacts to whom they may well be able to refer you.

---

and shiatsu will be able to tell you when the body's energies are back into better balance; and soon you will learn to know how this feels, and so be able to recognize when it is necessary to go back for 'top-up' sessions. It is certainly hoped that, by this time, your life and health will be onto a very much sounder footing, and that you will be experiencing the strong benefits of all the learning changes and self-discovery that you have made.

If you are following the year's programme at Bristol, try to commit yourself to the two follow-up days, as the boost to your motivation and morale will be invaluable. You will meet others that are further down the path than you, and they will by now be showing the benefits of sticking to their programme. You will also be surprised at how much your personal goal-posts have moved, and how much you are now able to fine-tune your programme and goals.

Regardless of whether you are able to come to Bristol and take part directly in the therapy programme, it is important to give yourself recognition for what you have achieved through adopting the Bristol Approach, and to have your progress recognized by the therapists that see you regularly. Embarking upon the holistic way of doing things is not the easy option; it would be far easier to stick your head in the sand or get on with 'life as normal'. It is therefore very good to take stock regularly so that you can really honour yourself for the work you have done and the progress you are making.

# 5

# *Making Self-Help Work for You*

First of all let me say again that it will be almost impossible to make any form of self-help work for you if your energy levels are low – below the conceptual 30 per cent line described in Chapter 2 as part of the energy model. So it is important to be realistic about whether you are yet in a position to start and sustain self-help activity. When you decide you have the strength and the stamina to get going – or if you have a good supporter who can do lots of the work for you – then these are some good practical tips that will help you to make sure that you don't fail.

## Healthy Eating

Because the subject of healthy eating is such a big one, the Bristol Cancer Help Centre's catering consultant, Jane Sen, and I have written books that explain the principles of healthy eating. My book, *Healing Foods* (*see* Further Reading), gives a straight-forward explanation of why it is important to change the way you eat if you have cancer, or if you want to prevent cancer. It explains how to do it step by step, so that the changes will be sustainable, and gives you a list of recommended foods, shopping lists, cooking guidelines and menu ideas for ideal meals. It also includes a section on the use of food as therapy or medicine in its own right. Jane Sen's *Healing Foods Cookbook* (*see* Further

Reading, and sample recipes in Appendix I), will help you to prepare and use these foods in an exciting and appetizing way.

The main emphasis in the Centre's dietary guidelines is to increase the amount of (preferably organic) vegetables and fruits in your diet whilst simultaneously reducing the amount of animal fat, meat, salt, sugary foods and processed foods to an absolute minimum. A typical day's healthy menu is shown in the box opposite. In principle, healthy eating will involve rebuilding your diet around wholefoods: pulses, nuts, seeds and the many different grains. To most of us this sounds very challenging, but with the help of Jane Sen, either directly or through reading her book, it can become a really creative pleasure, and you will discover how delicious this food can be.

One of the top tips for avoiding failure when changing your diet is to start by including more of the good things before getting rid of the others that are not good for you. For instance, you can first include vegetables or fruit in every meal; you can then begin to replace everything that is white with the brown equivalent, e.g. bread, rice, pasta and flour; and then you can begin to substitute vegetarian products for their animal counterparts – particularly butter, cheese, meat, cream and milk.

If you feel protein hungry and are not satisfied by vegetarian proteins it is best to eat some deep-sea fish (or fish that has not been farmed), have two to three eggs a week, and occasionally have some organic free-range meat (preferably chicken or game). It is also wise to drink plenty of high-quality water (around 2 litres/4 pints per day). If necessary this can taken as herbal tea.

Between meals – mid-morning, tea-time and mid-evening – it also good to make yourself fresh juice. To do this you will need to invest in a juice extractor, which can be obtained from electrical suppliers. The most basic models are centrifugal, which are adequate for the purpose. At the other end of the spectrum you will find juice-presses, which are thought to be less destructive of the plant enzymes but are about ten times the price of the centrifugal juicers.

## Sample menu for the day

*Breakfast*
- Organic muesli with soya milk, oat milk, rice milk or fruit juice.
- Fresh fruit salad or stewed fruit compote.
- Brown toast with soya margarine, honey or low-sugar jam
- Herb tea or fruit juice.
- An occasional organic free-range boiled egg with brown toast.

*Mid-morning*
- Freshly made juice.

*Lunch*
- Fresh salad with mixed leaves, sprouts, grated or chopped vegetables, nuts, seeds, dried fruits, or cooked beans with home-made salad dressing.
- Home-made vegetable soup, which could be fortified with pasta, barley or rice if desired.
- Wholefood pie or pasties.
- Fresh fruit.
- Fruit juice.
- Organic wholemeal brown bread with soya margarine.

*Mid-afternoon*
- Freshly made juice.

*Dinner*
- Mixed-leaf salad with home made vinaigrette.
- Vegetarian lentil shepherd's pie with steamed vegetables, e.g. carrots and broccoli.
- Baked bananas with cinnamon-date syrup, with soya cream, soya ice cream or soya yoghurt.
- Herb tea or coffee substitute.

If you take your vitamin and mineral supplements with these juices you will be supplying the body with the best possible blend of co-factors and plant enzymes to make the vitamins and minerals of maximum use to the body. The only exception to this is zinc, which is better taken without food, for example last thing before bed. This is because zinc tends to bind to other foods, making it harder for the body to absorb and use it.

Your vitamins can be obtained by mail order or by phone from the Cancer Help Centre Shop (*see* Appendix II). This method of obtaining your vitamins is easy and efficient, and there is the added advantage of knowing that you are benefiting the Centre's charity. Fine-tuning of your vitamin recommendations, and suggestions about other metabolic support, will be given by your holistic doctor at Bristol or elsewhere.

---

**Vitamin and mineral supplementation**

The Centre's basic recommendations for supplementation are:

- Vitamin C as calcium ascorbate: 2 g three times a day (build up to this level gradually).
- Beta-carotene: 15 mg per day (which is equivalent to 1½ pints/750 ml of carrot juice).
- Selenium: 200 micrograms per day.
- Zinc orotate: 100 mg per day reducing to 30 mg per day after three months
- Vitamin B complex: 50 mg per day.
- Vitamin E: 400 IU per day.

---

## Relaxation

Learning relaxation can initially be likened to reducing the idling speed on an engine that is revving too fast and therefore wasting precious fuel. If you are full of tension then a great deal of your precious vital energy is being wasted, especially during the frightening period after diagnosis and in the lead-up to treatments.

To start with it might be jolly difficult to learn to let go: as the modern-day adage has it, 'I can't possibly let go – its only my tension that's holding me together!' In these situations the best thing is to start by being relaxed passively by someone else: this can be done through massage, healing, shiatsu, or by being talked down into a relaxed state by a relaxation therapist, yoga teacher, or hypnotherapist. This will enable you to experience what relaxation feels like so that you know what you are aiming for. If you can't find a relaxation therapist in your area, enquire at your local health-food shops or natural health centres: they will usually know of a local yoga teacher who will probably be prepared to teach you relaxation.

It can be very useful to make a tape of your relaxation session with the therapist so that you can take it home and use it to help you repeat the deep relaxation exercise in between sessions with the therapist. Another possibility is that your supporter may wish to come along to your relaxation session to learn how to talk you down into a relaxed state. What some people have done to great effect, having learnt the principles, is made a tape of their own voice talking through a relaxation exercise. It is wonderful to hear your own voice telling you to relax and let go. This forms a great template for your new healing relationship with yourself.

If it is difficult for you to take up any of these options then the next best thing is to buy a relaxation tape. These are available from the Bristol Cancer Help Centre Shop and good health-food shops.

A day will come when you are sufficiently experienced in doing the relaxation exercises that you will no longer need a tape, but can take yourself naturally through the sequential releasing process. Soon after that you will find that it becomes quite easy and straightforward to switch straight into relaxation without even having to talk yourself down. Once you have developed this ability you can get used to going into the relaxation response at any time and in any situation where you suddenly find that you are holding unnecessary tension in the body.

Do not be surprised if you fall asleep when you first start to practise relaxation. Usually when we first start the process we quickly become aware of how absolutely exhausted we are beneath our 'coping façade'. Eventually, as your energy levels are raised, this will stop happening and you will be able to stay awake throughout the relaxation.

However, do remember overall that sleep is not the same as relaxation. Many people say to me, 'I have no problem at all relaxing, I can drop off the minute I sit down in a chair.' The reality is that despite the sleep, we can wake up as anxious as before: this is evident because analysis has shown that levels of the metabolites of the stress chemicals in our urine can be as high after sleep as they were before. So even if you are able to sleep it is also very important to learn relaxation. In some areas it is possible to join a relaxation class, and it may be helpful to contact the organization Relaxation For Living to see if there is a group in your area.

## Meditation

Before you embark upon learning meditation it is best to get to grips with relaxation. It is jolly difficult to try to still the mind when you are tense.

I would say that, for most people, learning meditation is easier in a group. The intense focus and very peaceful atmosphere generated by a group of people meditating is somewhat 'catching' and makes the process far easier. If you come to Bristol you will have the opportunity to experience learning meditation in a group. Alternatively you may like to find meditation classes in your area, and this can be done by contacting a transcendental meditation teacher, or the Friends of the Western Buddhist

Order; again, most yoga teachers will know where meditation classes are happening in their area. They may well be prepared to teach you meditation themselves. Alternatively your local health-food store or natural therapy centre may know.

A commitment to meditate regularly is the greatest possible gift you can give yourself because it can make an immense difference to both your health and your happiness. If someone else in your household wishes to join you in your meditation practice, this will be a great help as you will support and motivate each other.

## Spiritual Enquiry

During the residential week at the Cancer Help Centre the Centre's co-founder, Pat Pilkington, runs a session to help participants look at the very important spiritual questions that arise in the con-

---

### A space of your own

A very useful tip for getting your own meditation practice going at home is to create a meditation space in your house. Even if this is a corner of your bedroom, try to make a place where you can put your meditation cushion or chair and decorate your meditation space in a way that makes it feel like a sanctuary for you. This may mean plants, candles, flowers, pictures, crystals or special stones, feathers or twigs you have picked up.

If you make it a special place that feels lovely to be in, it will act as a tangible reminder of your intention to meditate and will draw you towards it. Then if you can make a set time every day, morning and evening, when you give yourself 20 minutes in your sanctuary, your meditation sessions can be as fixed a routine as brushing your teeth.

---

text of the diagnosis of cancer. If you are unable to come to Bristol, you should be able to find a group in your own community to whom you can turn for this sort of spiritual help.

If you do not already have firm religious convictions, you may find that this is a time when you wish to explore, or revive, religious ideas or beliefs. Many find the Buddhist or Christian perspectives helpful as neither of these traditions views death as final, and many find the tranquillity in the silence of Quaker meetings immensely valuable. Or you may – as many who have come to Bristol have found – want to define your personal spirituality and beliefs, based on the insights and wisdom that come to you through the process of working with the holistic healing approach.

Quite often, as the spiritual realm becomes opened up to you in this healing process, learnt beliefs fall away and are replaced by a more gnostic sense of what is true to you.

## Visualization and Affirmation

In developing your personal visualization, it is helpful if you can work with a counsellor who can help you make sure that your chosen visualization is as complete and as appropriate as possible.

If you don't have a counsellor, or the opportunity to use one, then it is a good idea to get hold of a book on visualization. The ones I would recommend are *Getting Well Again*, by Carl Simonton, *Sun Over Mountain*, by Jessica McBeth, or *Creative Visualization*, by Shakti Gawain (*see* Further Reading). You will see tapes on visualization being advertised but these usually take you through the process of guided visualization. This means that the voice on the tape will lead you through a very pleasant journey aimed at getting you into a much better frame of mind. This is very beneficial, but it is a completely different process from personal visualization.

In using personal visualization or imagery, you are trying to achieve five things:

1. To get an image of the cancer itself – its nature, colour or texture. This does not have to be biologically accurate. Some people have seen their cancers as blocks of ice or spiky conkers, others as specks of sand or lumps of jelly. It is entirely up to you.

2. To imagine an agent that would completely remove the cancer from the body. Here it is important to make sure that the agent you choose is actually strong enough to do this. Every time you go about removing the cancer from the body in your mind's eye, make sure that it is all gone.

3. To see yourself whole and healed. To do this some people like to see themselves being washed through with healing love, light, water, a gentle breeze, or perhaps a specific colour, or any other image that they find deeply healing or transformative.

4. Another possibility is to form an image of yourself as very strong and powerful. This image might be a 'power animal', like a mighty eagle or lion, or an inanimate power symbol, such as the Statue of Liberty – whatever image or symbol has power for you.

5. To add even more power to this process it is good to visualize yourself alive and well at important events in the future.

Some people find it quite difficult to conjure up pictures in their mind's eye and prefer to do it in words or affirmations, which they repeat to themselves. For this process you can simply close your eyes and say, for example:

- 'I see myself completely well and totally clear of cancer.'
- 'I feel healing love and light flowing through my body, restoring complete health in all my tissues and cells.'

- 'I choose to be present in five years' time at my son's graduation'

Or whatever feels right for you in your own words; the important thing is that you draw the power of these choices into your body as you speak.

You can apply this process to very much more mundane things to achieve the outcomes you want in any other sort of situation – deciding that your bank balance will become more positive, for example. It sounds crazy but in fact this 'mind over matter' technique has been known and practised for a very long time in sport and business with phenomenal effects.

Through visualization we create a scenario that requires us to be alive, well and present in the future, and we effectively undo the negative affirmatory process, which may have occurred during the diagnosis of cancer when you may have received powerful messages about how long you are likely to survive.

As you begin to refine this process you can even use it to make choices on a moment to moment basis, when things are not going your way. For example, if you find yourself in the middle of an argument, you can stop and make the choice that the conversation will end harmoniously with a positive outcome. You will be very surprised and delighted by the effectiveness of this technique.

## Exercise

Try if you can to start each day with a stretching session:

- Stand with your feet hip-width apart and stretch your arms up, first one side then the other, pointing the toe on the opposite side simultaneously.
- Then rotate your shoulders in their joints to loosen the shoulder muscles. Gently rotate your neck, applying a little lift to the head as you do so in order that you do not stress

the vertebrae in the neck. (The head is a lot heavier than you think.)

- Next put the feet about 1 m (40 in) apart; allow yourself to bend forward, and put your hands on the floor. If it is comfortable, place one hand in the central position and then, twisting your spine, lift the other arm above your head, and look upwards. Repeat on the other side. Be gentle with yourself – do not go past your comfortable limit.

- From this position go onto all fours, and then stretch the spine like a cat, first of all upwards – tucking your chin into your chest – and then dipping or hollowing your back and extending your head and neck upwards and backwards. Once you have the hang of this, give some attention to your breathing at the same time: inhale as you hollow your spine, and exhale as you arch your back upwards. Repeat this process very slowly and smoothly, and really enjoy the feeling.

- Then, if you are able, come to a sitting position on the floor, and gently bend forward into your maximum stretch position without any pushing or pulling or straining of the muscles.

- Then uncurl gently, and lie flat on the floor for a few minutes so that you can absorb the benefits of these stretches.

- Then, if you are game, support your lower back with your hands and swing your legs up into a shoulder stand. Remain inverted for several minutes, trying to relax into this position. Then, again, uncurl gently, vertebra by vertebra and lie still again on the floor for a few minutes before you get up.

Just these simple stretches will invigorate you no end, making it much easier to do all your other self-help activity.

An audio tape, made by Tessa Morgan, on daily yoga practice is obtainable from the Cancer Help Centre. On its B side are exercises that can be done seated in a chair or even in bed if necessary. In addition to this stretching routine, try to include a walk or swim, and opportunities for plenty of fresh air, as part of your weekly routine. Ideally, once you are able, add a regular visit to a yoga, t'ai chi or chi gong class, and you will soon experience great benefits from increasing your physical activity. Over time, your energy levels will increase so much that you will find your need for therapy will drop away. At this stage you will be strong enough to motivate yourself to maintain this self-help activity, and will go from strength to strength.

---

## A basic day plan

A good structure for your daily programme would be:

**A.M.**

| | |
|---|---|
| 7.00–7.15 | Stretching |
| 7.15–7.45 | Relaxation and meditation |
| 8.00–9.00 | Wholefood breakfast plus vitamins and mineral supplements |
| 11.00 | Freshly made vegetable juice with wholefood biscuits and fruit |

**P.M.**

| | |
|---|---|
| 1.00 | Wholefood lunch, plus vitamins and minerals |
| 4.00 | Freshly made juice, with wholefood cake or biscuits |
| 7.00–8.00 | Wholefood dinner, plus vitamins and minerals |
| 9.00–9.30 | Meditation |
| 9.30 | Freshly made vegetable juice |
| 10.00 | Zinc tablet. Relaxing bath, with candles and oils; bedtime |

---

# 6

# *When the Going Gets Tough ...*

One could almost say that the very definition of crisis is that you forget what help and resources you have at your disposal, either personally, through family and friends, or via professionals. Inevitably, from time to time on your cancer journey, you will 'lose the plot', wondering if you have achieved anything at all through your holistic endeavours. At such a crisis point, it is important to get help from your therapists and/or counsellors. If you are taking part in Bristol's therapy programme, a follow-up visit to the Centre would be appropriate. You can also get help over the phone from the Cancer Centre's helpline, the follow-up nurse or the doctor phone-in.

It is at such times of crisis that the work you put in during your initial explorations of the holistic approach will pay off immensely. If you have located a good counsellor, healer and energy therapist in your area, they will be there in the background if things become difficult for you again. This means that you can quickly step up the level of support, knowing not only that these good people are close at hand but also that they already know you well and will be able to go straight to the point.

Troubled times can give new impetus to your therapy, taking it to a new, deeper level, which can bring great rewards. The trigger to restart your therapy may come either because of problems in your personal life, because of new symptoms of the illness or side-effects from treatment, or because you have been told you have a recurrence. Whether or not it is cancer-related, if you recognize that you have become stressed or distressed then it is time to step up the level of help again.

It is also at difficult times that you will benefit especially from having put time and energy into learning relaxation, meditation and visualization. This remains true even if you are suddenly panicked or thrown into confusion or pain, and feel that these skills have completely deserted you. This is the point at which to loop back round and start the support process all over again, although, in reality, it won't seem that you are starting all over again because it will be like revisiting old friends rather than meeting new people. Once you are back in your support group, relaxation or meditation class, or working with your counsellor on the process of visualization, it will all come back to you very quickly; and, again, the opportunity will be there to deepen and intensify your practice.

## Keeping in Touch

If you have been through counselling once, and gone quite fully into the holistic approach, you might feel that you have 'been there, done that', and therefore reached a point at which there is nothing more to do. In fact this is very far from the truth, and it is good to remember Penny Brohn's most pertinent comment that 'healing is a process and not an event'. Much as we would wish it otherwise, life and cancer can throw us googlies at any time, knocking us off balance. The most important thing is that you do not deny yourself access to your therapist. Do not fall back into the old habit of thinking that you cannot justify spending the money on yourself in this way, or that you have taken quite enough of their time and attention in the past, or that you had better just buckle down and get on with life.

Once again, it is about recognizing your state and evaluating your needs (discussed in Chapter 2). Try to do this at any point when your equilibrium is disturbed. Get used to tuning in to how you really feel, taking time to settle down and get in touch with what is going on with your body, your mind, and your spirit. You may wish to ask your higher self for insight and guidance: imagine yourself as your own guardian angel, looking at yourself with great love, and seeing from this compassionate perspective more clearly what is needed.

In fact, it is a good idea to get into the habit of tuning into your state regularly (*see* box below), either alone, or with a loved one or friend, so that you get better and better at seeing what is

---

### Tuning in

If you find it difficult to 'let go' sufficiently to be able to explore and 'feel' your feelings, it can help if you actively set the stage for it. The way of doing this will vary from person to person, but as time goes on you will discover what works best for you. You could try, for example, running yourself a hot, perfumed bath, lighting a candle, and playing some emotionally cathartic music. In these safe but evocative surroundings you can really allow yourself to cry or groan, 'bottoming out' with your pain, distress and anguish.

At first this might seem a scary thing to do: you might feel that if you begin to let go, there will be no end to the release of the feelings stored up inside, and that you will fall into a bottomless pit. However, most people find that after a good ten-minute cry, or a five-minute, full-blast rant, there is very little else to come out. Afterwards, you can enjoy the feeling of 'peace after the storm' when you can 'cuddle' and soothe yourself in a very gentle way, perhaps by curling up under your duvet or by getting a friend to hold or stroke you.

---

going on underneath the coping front that you show the world. This will enable you to adjust your activities and expectations accordingly (if this is necessary), and organize life around your current needs and feelings. Remember that your feelings are always subject to change, and outer adjustments, as such, are not always necessary.

## Communicating with others

When you are in extremis it is easy to forget to communicate properly with others about how you are feeling and what you need. Keeping communication going is vital, even if it is only to tell everybody to leave you alone for a few hours.

If you have made a support group of personal friends around you this can be a very good time to call an emergency support group meeting in order for them to give you the emotional holding you require to express your feelings. Most people feel the need of the presence of others in order to express their emotions, feeling unable to do it on their own in the way described in the box on page 105. At these times you will recognize the value of having built your personal support team prior to getting into difficulties, as it is very hard to make this kind of practical arrangement when you are in trouble.

Of course the other thing to remember is that if you are going through a difficult time, those close to you are also very likely to feel frightened and upset, and will need support in their own right. The quicker that each of you can take your distress outside of the family or home situation to professional helpers, the quicker the tension levels in the home will start to settle, helping the crisis to pass rather than to escalate.

## Bringing help to you

Sometimes there are practical problems that prevent your being able to get to therapists, groups or classes, and at these times the absent healing services of the National Federation of Spiritual Healers (NFSH) and the White Eagle Lodge (*see* Appendix II) can be invaluable. These organizations can be contacted either by phone or in writing. They will ask you for the details of your situation, and then at regular intervals the group of healers who meet to send absent healing will concentrate on sending healing to you. If you have mentioned that those around you are also in trouble, they will send healing to those people as well. Almost always this extraordinary intervention makes a very great difference to your morale, and other help can begin to come in unexpected ways.

It may be that your own healer or therapists are in a position to visit your home; if they are not, the NFSH or White Eagle referral services may be able to find a healer who can visit you.

Sometimes a good source of help can be your local church. Even if you are not religious, the local vicar or senior church members are usually very glad to visit the homes of those who are ill or suffering; they are happy just to be there for you, giving comfort or conducting prayer or services in the house if you would like that. It is also possible to ask friends or your local church to set up a prayer circle for you.

Another very important thing to remember is to pray yourself. Even if you have never prayed in your life before, try asking very specifically for the help you need. Allow yourself to surrender to a force that is greater than you and that can bring you help at your time of need. You may very well be surprised by what can start to come towards you if you let go in this way, and allow yourself to ask for the help you need so badly.

In real extremis the other organization that is absolutely invaluable is the Samaritans, who are there to talk to anyone who is completely at the end of their tether, whatever the problem. You can also obtain help from your GP, the practice nurses, the local MacMillan or Marie Curie service, the local hospice or the specialist counsellors on your cancer unit. Don't forget that these services are not set up only for people who are terminally ill or in the midst of a medical emergency; they are available for you whatever difficulties you are experiencing. This is particularly true of modern–day hospices, which usually aim to provide help and support for people with cancer in a whole host of practical and social ways from the point of diagnosis onwards.

## Keeping Control

When the going gets tough the most important thing is to try not to lose yourself or 'give away your power'. The best way to keep control of your medical situation is by asking for time to think about what it is you want to do about whatever it is that is being offered to you. This gives you the chance to go through your emotional reaction, gather information, to visit your holistic doctor, or chat with an holistic doctor via the doctor phone-in at the Bristol Cancer Help Centre (*see* Chapter 9), to seek a sec-ond opinion medically if necessary, and, most important of all, to work out what it is that is right for you in the situation.

If you feel that not enough is being done, or that your med-ical team has 'written you off', it is sometimes possible to secure more help by approaching the problem from a different angle. For example, when Penny Brohn's oncology team felt that they could offer no more treatment for her spinal tumour she sought the opinion of an orthopedic surgeon. When he felt he could offer no help she sought the opinion of a neuro-surgeon. The neuro-surgeon leapt into gallant action, performing surgery to decompress the trapped spinal nerves, which were the cause of her increasing difficulty in walking. As a result, Penny had three more years of mobility, and this allowed her to renovate a beau-tiful mountainside cottage in Crete with her husband David; she created many gorgeous mosaics on the walls and floors, thor-oughly enjoying and expressing herself in the process. Without her persistent, lateral approach, she would probably have been bedridden at home or in a hospice receiving palliative care.

As Penny's experiences show, knowing which options can be pursued is part of the battle, and this can be helped considerably if you have a good GP or holistic doctor ally.

Another door that can open more fully the harder you push is access to pain management. Usually cancer pain is managed by the GP or palliative care team, but if this is not working it may be time to seek the help of an anaesthetist. Most big cities have pain clinics within their hospitals' departments of anaesthesis, and these can offer very sophisticated pain management, which is beyond the scope of most oncology services. For example, if pain has become chronic and unbearable it may be possible for an anaesthetist to perform a permanent pain-block.

## Keeping Going

Sometimes it is the nights that are the hardest to bear. You may feel reluctant to disturb your family, and may already have had to decamp into another room to sleep so as not to disturb your partner. This can be especially miserable if you are then unable to sleep either because of pain, fear or simply because of relative inactivity or steroid treatment. It is very helpful to get yourself set up with distractions such as a portable television, a lap-top computer through which you can access the Internet, or even simply a notebook and pen with which you can begin writing a journal of what you are feeling and thinking, as these very quiet periods are often times of great clarity and poignancy.

The other approach you can take is to try to organize a rota of friends who will come and sit with you through the night. They might well find this a surprisingly rewarding time, allowing them to deepen their relationship with you and catch more of a glimpse of what it is you are really going through. Here, again, it is a question of being brave enough to ask for what you need.

If you are not in a position to provide yourself with technological distractions or friends who will sit with you, another good plan is to obtain a personal stereo with headphones so that you can use these times to listen to beautiful music or poetry, or even to the whole books that are increasingly available on tape and CD for use by the blind.

If you do become limited in your activity, the great challenge is to keep on living creatively within your new limitations rather than getting stuck in the state of grieving for what you have lost. Of course, this can usually happen only after a period of appropriate grieving but, none the less, it is important to try to make the transition so that you can fully express and enjoy yourself within your new limits. This is easier said than done, and it is very hard not to feel bitter and depressed when things seem to be getting progressively harder. I can honestly say though, that I have witnessed many people who, given the right level of psychological and spiritual support, have kept on rising to and overcoming the new challenges, and who have continued to find the humour and opportunity in the difficulties whilst developing ever sweeter, more poignant relationships with themselves and those who care for them.

# 7

# *Caring for the Carers*

Over the years of working as an holistic doctor, I have had the opportunity of asking people with serious illness which of their traumatic life events they feel have most affected their own health. A very frequent reply has been looking after a relative or close person with cancer or other serious illness. This alerted me to the vulnerability of those that are in the supporting role, and led in 1998 to a change of policy at Bristol: to offer places on the Centre's courses for people in the supporting role on an exactly equal footing to those they are caring for.

In the past, supporters of people with cancer were always invited to attend the Bristol Cancer Help Centre with their friend or partner with cancer, but this was in a passive role. The main reason for the carers' being there was to help to provide any practical help that was needed and to help in the process of gathering new information and learning the various self-help skills in order to re-enforce the practice of the person with cancer once they got home. In the past the Centre ran groups within all of its courses for supporters to begin to explore their state and needs. However it became clear that this was really just scratching the surface of the problem – that in reality the supporters needed counselling, healing, body work, and even appointments with doctors in their own right.

Many carers suffer from acute anxiety or intense grief, not to mention confusion about the complex set of feelings they are experiencing. Whilst wishing dearly to 'get it right' for loved ones, many are troubled by feelings of guilt because underneath a reasonably calm exterior they might feel considerable anger or resentment at finding themselves in this new role, suddenly expected to reorientate themselves and their life around an illness. Many struggle with whether or not they can maintain their relationships in the face of the new demand, whilst others feel neglected and themselves abandoned by their partner, who is receiving a great deal of attention, albeit for a very difficult reason. Probably the most common feeling of all is an immense desire to be able to make things better or to make the pain go away whilst at the time feeling a deep sense of inadequacy and impotence at being unable to achieve this. Sometimes carers have confessed that they wished their partner could die more quickly so that they personally do not have to keep experiencing such terrible emotional pain.

Of course, these feelings are often mixed with a wonderful sense of new closeness created by dealing so intimately with each other's needs and vulnerability, and there is often a rekindling of great love between partners faced with the possibility of being separated. Many feel very fulfilled in the role of carer, some even feeling that it has brought new purpose and meaning to their lives.

Overall, most people tend to swing between these poles, finding the combination of the emotional intensity, physical and financial demands, added pressures of taking on some of the other's tasks, getting to and from medical appointments, as well as holding down a job and dealing with the emotional upheaval in the immediate social circle, utterly exhausting.

Another problem is that, almost inevitably, the carer and the person with cancer try to protect each other from the full impact of what they are feeling physically and emotionally. This can lead to a protective impasse or double bind, which limits communication and damages relationships. Many carers have said that their own emotional state tends to mirror that of the person they are caring for, and so they can feel happy and relaxed only when their close one is feeling this way. This leaves them feeling like a cork bobbing about on a sea of emotion, very much at the mercy of what is happening to their partner. Some cope by seeking refuge outside the house, taking trips alone or with friends, or 'escaping' to the cinema or theatre in order to get a break from the emotional intensity. Many feel that they can never get the pressure of the cancer out of their minds, and whilst some welcome the lifestyle changes that the cancer can bring with it (especially when the person with cancer makes positive changes through the use of the holistic approach), others resent these bitterly.

The other side of the story is that people with cancer often complain that their carer is inhibiting their emotional expression because they are obviously fed up and no longer able to cope. They also speak about feelings of suffocation from the over-protectiveness of partners, saying that from the moment of diagnosis they have been handled with kid gloves.

From listening to carers talking in this way, it became clear to us at the Cancer Help Centre that they themselves were very vulnerable because of a combination of stress, exhaustion, emotional conflict, and the lack of opportunity to express their feelings. It was also apparent that often the relationships between carers and those they cared were deteriorating because of communication difficulties. This, combined with the social limitations placed on somebody who is increasingly confined to the home base in a care-giving role, puts them at risk of developing stress-related illness themselves, as well as making it likely that their social and professional life will suffer.

## Getting Help

Whilst the provision of support services for people with cancer in the NHS is patchy to say the least, the provision of support services for carers is non-existent. There is some minimal recognition by the Government of the role of care-givers in the family amongst the chronically physically or mentally disabled, but almost no recognition of the role families play in looking after somebody who has cancer. This makes it even more vital that people in the care-giving role think very clearly about their own needs and well-being.

If you are a carer, start by temporarily taking your attention off the loved one. Seek the support of a holistic doctor and counsellor, and begin to feel properly the effect that the diagnosis of cancer in one so close has had upon you. For some people this is easier done independently, i.e., without the presence of their partner. (For this reason, some carers come to Bristol, or undertake counselling elsewhere, on their own.)

The next thing – in exactly the same way as it is for the person with cancer (whether at Bristol or not) – is to go through the process of recognizing your own state and needs and being helped to do this by holistic doctors, counsellors and healers. If you are able to attend Bristol's five-day residential course you will also receive body work, and will be encouraged to learn the self-help skills of relaxation and meditation so that you can practise these regularly at home in order to protect yourself from the effects of stress. If you are not coming to Bristol, try to get similar help in your home area.

You can use this time to unburden yourself emotionally and to check with a doctor that your physical health is holding up. Or you can go further, seizing the opportunity that the crisis has given you to think about making lifestyle changes that would be even more protective long term. In this way you can engage in a process that mirrors that of the person you are supporting, and you can become equally excited about the possibilities of making important life-enhancing changes.

Once you have laid these foundations, either through attending Bristol's residential week or through the help of your local holistic doctor, the most pressing need is to establish regular counselling on a weekly or fortnightly basis. It can also be helpful to have regular healing or massage to deal with the effects of tension and exhaustion.

It is important not to forget the effects on other members of the household, too. Children can also be feeling the effects of the stress and distress much more than they say, or even realize themselves. Veronica Mills, who was quoted in Chapter 3, found that she coped with this by asking her own counsellor to do one session a month at the family home with all members of the family present. This gave her children and husband a chance to 'empty out' their feelings on a regular basis. It included once, she told me, her young son's expressing his fury that she was getting a new juicer when he couldn't have a new BMX bike! More serious than this, though, they were enabled to speak freely about their worst fears, talking openly about what it would be like if she died, which gave them all the chance to express their deep love for each other.

It is important that carers and their partners are given separate, confidential counselling sessions so that they can feel comfortable about expressing their feelings. It is also a good idea to have a session together in which your communication and relationship issues are looked at too. This can be particularly important where new problems have arisen since the diagnosis, or you both feel that there have been long-standing communication or relationship problems that may have contributed to the illness's developing in the first place.

Whether or not you are able to go to Bristol for this kind of counselling and support, it is important for you to set up your own support system at in your home area so that you can access help regularly. A local counsellor can be found through the Centre for Transpersonal Psychology or the British Association of Counsellors, and a healer through the National Federation of Spiritual Healers or the White Eagle Lodge (*see* Appendix II). You may well be inclined to think that you don't need this, or that all the family resources should go towards helping the person with cancer. But it is very important to remember what has been said in Chapter 3 about the way that distress ricochets around the family.

Your part in helping to prevent this ricochet effect is in making sure that you are helped to express your distress and pain outside the family system. By doing this you will be a better supporter to the one you are caring for because you will have cleared your own emotional decks. It is also vital that you are protected through what may be a long and complex process. You may also find that you actually grow and benefit from the process, and become closer to the one you love rather than gradually becoming submerged beneath your feelings, hiding from yourself and your partner, and becoming depressed, embittered and progressively more unavailable – all of which makes it far more likely that you will end up with stress-related illness yourself.

These ideas and suggestions are summarized in the carer survival plan below.

## Carer survival plan

### Get emotional support

- Get yourself a local counsellor. Set up regular visits, even if these are at relatively long intervals, and go for your sessions even if you don't think you need them.
- Set yourself up with a personal support team distinct from that of your partner. Meet regularly with your team so that you can talk freely about your needs and what you are going through.
- Get joint counselling help if your relationship with the person you are caring for is getting into difficulties.

### Take space and time for you

- Make sure that you don't lose or abandon yourself in the process of looking after the person you are caring for. Create your own private space in the house, and mark out times during the week when you can be on your own – either in or out of the house – pursuing entirely your own interests, or simply resting and relaxing.

**Stay fit**
- Exercise regularly two or three times a week. Make at least one of these times exercise in the fresh air. If possible make another of these times a yoga or t'ai chi class. Perhaps the third could be a swim or some other form of aerobic exercise.
- Eat well; if possible, adopt the Bristol's healthy eating approach, along with your partner.
- Take supplements. It is advisable to take 50 mg of Vitamin B Complex per day and 500 mg of Vitamin C three times daily, as well as a multivitamin/mineral tablet to protect you from the effects of stress.

**Develop a spiritual practice**
- If at all possible commit yourself to learning to meditate. This will give you the inner strength you need to help you to continue to cope with your situation, as well as benefiting you in other areas of your life.

**Keep communicating**
- Schedule special times with the person you are supporting so that you can let each other know exactly how you are feeling. This can be very difficult, so it helps if it is done in a structured way: take a specific amount of uninterrupted time each, just to say how you feel. It is immensely tempting to butt in, especially if you feel criticized, or think you have a solution, or simply want to make the other person feel better; but it is far more beneficial – for both of you – if you allow each other the space to talk, cry, shout, or do whatever else you need to do, uninterrupted. It is useful to set a boundary on this exercise by putting a limit on the time for each person to talk. If, through this process, you identify problems that cannot be sorted out between you, take these to a joint counselling session. Ideally your joint counsellor should not be the counsellor either of you are seeing individually as this can

interfere with your individual counselling and unfairly bias the support given.

- Don't forget to keep similar communication lines open with other people that are close to you both, or involved in the supporting role.

## Take regular breaks

- As hard as it may seem, it is important for you to get away regularly so that both of you have a rest from the dynamics of the relationship and overall situation. If the person you are looking after is very ill then it may be possible to do this by getting a member of their personal support team to come and stay whilst you are away. It may be possible for the person who is ill to have breaks away from the home base, too, so that this strategy feels balanced.

## Keep your own creative focus going

- Try not to abandon your own projects or creative ideas. You will be far more helpful and fun to be around if you are being stimulated and enjoying life.

## Keep a journal

- Difficult though this period may be, it is a special time of heightened insight and personal growth. Recording your thoughts and feelings is a protective and liberating exercise.

## Ask for help

- Do not try to keep everything going on your own. Recognize when you are getting tired, upset or overwhelmed and ask friends or healthcare professionals for help.
- Remember to pray, too, asking God or the universe to give you the strength you need to meet your challenge.

# 8

# *Integrating Holistic and Orthodox Medicines*

## Getting the Best out of Orthodox Medicine

*Help with the decision-making process*

Within the world of orthodox cancer medicine, things usually start to happen the minute a diagnosis of cancer is made. Many of the people that come to the Cancer Help Centre describe this immediate-action response to their diagnosis as 'like being hit by a steam train'. Often, people are presented – during the same conversation in which they are given their diagnosis and prognosis – with a complex choice of surgical, chemotherapeutic and radiotherapeutic options. Not infrequently, consent for these treatments to begin is elicited at the same time – when the individual is in a state of profound shock and distress.

Studies have shown repeatedly that from the moment the word 'cancer' is first spoken, people hardly ever retain a single other word that is said in that conversation. This means that more often than not consent for treatments to be implemented is being elicited during conversations that people don't even recall. Not only is there no time allowed for the person to absorb the shock, but there is no time made available for the intense emotional reaction that follows before treatments are

119

embarked upon, or for any support to be given. This means that individuals are usually starting treatments in the worst possible frame of mind – absolutely terrified, full of emotion, and without having given truly informed consent.

It is dangerous to subject people to complex and challenging medical procedures when they are very frightened and emotional, for it is when a person is in this state of high, sympathetic nervous-system arousal that the body is least able to re-equilibrate itself, heal and repair itself, fight infection, or achieve proper clotting of blood. Nursing studies have shown that patients that approach treatment or surgery with a calm state of mind, and that are in possession of all the facts and feeling empowered, have far fewer complications, require less pain-killing medication, and suffer far less psychologically, before, during and after treatment.

Because of the way that diagnosis and treatment for cancer is currently carried out, many people 'come to' several weeks after finishing their treatment, wondering what on earth has happened to them. The shock of the diagnosis and the trauma of the loss of their limb, breast or organ hits them, and a new grieving process begins. Sometimes this is coupled with the extra shock of losing hair or nervous sensation. Far more serious than this, some people discover at this point that they have been sterilized by the chemotherapy. Further down the line still, they may discover that the treatments that they were told were so imperative have in fact minimal chances of changing their prognosis – only extending the disease-free interval. And they may also find out about other worrying side-effects that are associated with the treatment they have received.

There are many times when having medical treatment is the right thing to do, but this should always take place when an individual has had sufficient chance to recover from the shock and upset of diagnosis, and he or she is able to hear and properly understand what is being said by others. This is important even if it means repeating key medical information many times.

Ideally, treatment should not be commenced until truly informed consent has been obtained, and the individual feels confident and right about the treatment being undertaken. It is better still if positive associations and feelings towards the treatment have been developed before the treatment starts, so that the individual does not embark on it while harbouring the very frightening, negative images that most people have in connection with chemotherapy and radiotherapy.

## The holistic doctor

The decision-making process is one of the areas in which holistic doctors can be very useful. The first thing they will do is review the medical situation, taking time to explain exactly what is going on medically and what the treatments offered really involve. They will compare these with other options that may be available, and look fully at the possible implications of not having treatment.

This process of review can be important when people have, as an immediate reaction, flatly refused any medical treatment when in fact at least some surgical intervention may well prevent disagreeable complications. On the other hand, saying no to treatment may be the wiser option if the disease is very advanced (and treatments can realistically promise only very minor improvement with a great loss of quality of life), and if sufficient inner strength can be cultivated to enable the individual to cope without treatment.

The key here is to insist that medical personnel allow sufficient time for you to think about these major decisions, so that you can become adjusted, motivated, properly prepared, and, ultimately, strongly committed to a particular course of action.

Often, time with the holistic doctor can help an individual formulate – and develop the confidence to ask – the key questions during subsequent medical consultations. Whatever else happens, it is vital to make sure that you are not being rushed, even if it seems to some that you are being slow and obstinate.

Remember that the medical profession are there to serve your needs and not the other way around.

## Getting what you need

This issue of taking charge does not apply only to the decision-making process with regard to treatments. It is very important that you take, and retain, similar control during all your interactions with the medical profession. Believe it or not, after the scientific study that showed that 'difficult' patients live longer, one support group in America had T-shirts printed with the legend 'I am a difficult patient' for people to wear on their trips to hospital.

By and large the British tend to be very passive in the face of authority, and to cherish a belief in the power of the medical profession to take care of us and sort everything out if we become ill. For many people, the cancer diagnosis is their first experience of the medical system outside the GP's surgery. For these people, it can be very disillusioning to realize both how relatively impotent even the highest-tech cancer medicine is, and the extent to which getting the choices, care and treatment you need is often a question of how assertive you are.

As daunting as it may seem it is important to step back from the advice that you receive from your own particular hospital consultant or unit and try to look at what is going on in the bigger picture, not just nationally but world wide, with respect to your type of cancer. Advances in conventional treatment continue to be made so, ideally, you should make sure that you are fully aware of all the current treatments and that there are no other options you could be exploring. The ways in which you can go about collecting this kind of information are discussed in the medical information section in Chapter 3 (*see* pages 61–3).

It is even more important, and perhaps even harder, to wake up early on after diagnosis to the fact that cancer medicine does not currently have all the answers or hope of cure in other than three of the relatively rare cancers: testicular cancer and some of the leukaemias and lymphomas. This means that what the medical profession has to offer, which is extremely important in controlling the unpleasant manifestations of the disease, should be viewed realistically – as one part of your holistic cancer plan; it should definitely not be passively relied upon to get you better.

Ideally, you should be striving for the best possible medical treatment with the highest possible degree of individualization of your care. This means ensuring that:

- You are given time to recover from the shock of diagnosis or bad news before being expected to think about treatment decisions.
- Treatment decisions are made with reference to all the relevant information (having consulted several sources).
- Your needs for support and counselling throughout the processes have been provided for. (If the medical unit that you are dealing with does not have facilities for this they should direct you to organizations, local or national, who can help.)
- You have been advised about other support agencies relevant to your particular illness or its treatment.
- Prior to making medical treatment decisions, you have access to information about the full range of alternative, complementary and mind–body options available in Britain and abroad, with (if possible) guidance on their use.

## Communicating with healthcare professionals

In the most crucial situations, the main thing that will make a difference to whether or not you get what you want is how well you are able to communicate with healthcare professionals, namely your consultant, your GP, and key nursing staff. This in turn will depend upon the openness and preparedness of medical personnel to take your views on board and to cater to your needs. It will help you to know that in the policy framework for commissioning cancer services – published by Doctors Calman and Hine, and known as the Calman Hine Report of 1995[22] – the second of the key recommendations and action points is:

The needs of patients and their carers should be the primary concern of purchasers, planners and professionals involved in cancer services.

The fourth of seven key principles that should govern the provision of cancer care is that:

> ...the development of cancer services should be patient-centred and should take account of patients', families' and carers' views and preferences as well as those of professionals involved in cancer care. Individuals' perceptions of their needs may differ from those of the professional. Good communication between professionals and patients is especially important.

If you are not sure how your team should be helping to establish, and provide for, your needs, it is worth consulting the Calman Hine Report, which outlines good practice.

---

### The feedback loop

Currently we are in a period of unprecedented commitment to 'user involvement' in the planning of healthcare services. Both at the primary care group level, and at the hospital-based cancer services level, all units are developing services based on the views of users.

It is therefore essential that if you find the services wanting you communicate your feelings either to the patient representatives in these planning bodies, or to the bodies directly, so that you, and others that follow, will see sustainable improvement based on your actual needs and not the perceived needs as defined by the medical profession.

---

# Using the Holistic Approach in Preparation for Treatment

You may experience some opposition to the idea from health-care professionals, but you can be sure that all studies that have been done on the subject show that adequately preparing people for treatments, both psychologically and physically – by providing information, by relaxation, or by teaching techniques to minimize the degree of distress involved – significantly reduces side-effects and the risk of post-treatment complications, while simultaneously improving treatment toleration and even the chances of survival.[7,8]

A great deal can also be done to prepare yourself nutritionally and physically. All treatments – surgical, chemotherapeutic and radiotherapeutic – are tolerated better if you are in a good state nutritionally. Those who have embarked upon the latter two treatments before and after adopting a healthy diet say that the difference is remarkable. When the body is in a less toxic state, the toxicity of these treatments is tolerated far better. Indeed there are studies that show that these treatments are enhanced by nutritional supplementation.[23] Good nutrition is also extremely helpful in preparing the body for surgery. Most surgical procedures involve a period of having nothing to eat – 'nil by mouth' – and of course an extensive period of recovery afterwards when sometimes the appetite is low or it is difficult to eat. To help your body cope with this, vitamin and mineral supplementation should ideally start immediately after diagnosis, as should any other improvements in diet to prepare the ground.

Lastly, your emotional state should be considered all the way through the treatment process. The treatment itself can produce depression or anxiety, and this may build up over time. This, coupled with exhaustion or physical side-effects, may mean that you become too vulnerable to receive treatment on certain days before you have received some emotional support. It is very important that both you and your healthcare professionals are sensitive to this, and that you ask for some help or recovery time if you need it before continuing with treatment. People who do not acknowledge their own sense of vulnerability, or who ignore their inner voice saying Stop, and continue with treatment when they know they can't really cope with it, can find themselves plunged into psychological or physical crisis.

## Complementary Therapies in the Clinical Setting

The main value of complementary therapies in the clinical setting is in supportive care and symptom management. The idea is to use therapies or remedies that will reduce symptoms directly, or to learn techniques that will help to alleviate symptoms as they arise. Symptoms invariably have three components:

- The physical level of the symptom.
- The fear and anxiety that the symptom creates (and that usually exacerbates it).
- The emotional response to the symptom (which is very often repressed and can make the symptom worse).

Holistic or complementary symptom management is therefore usually directed at addressing each of these levels independently.

First, attempts are made to relieve anxiety and fear by helping you to talk about your fears as well as helping you to learn relaxation techniques. Methods used to relax you can include massage, hypnotherapy, as well as soothing breathing techniques, aromatherapy, or simply being talked down into a relaxed state. Second, there is a need to facilitate emotional expression or catharsis, and this is often made possible if a sufficiently empathic bond has been established between you and the carer, and you feel able to 'let go'. Very often, the degree to which symptoms are reduced as a result of relaxation and emotional expression is so great that either the symptom becomes entirely manageable or it can be controlled by smaller levels of conventional drugs or by natural medicines. Third, specific therapies, such as acupuncture, reflexology, shiatsu, or the use of homoeopathic and herbal remedies, are used in order to manage the physical aspect of the symptom.

Another approach can be to use the mind itself either to change or to transcend the symptom. With the former, conscious attention is focused directly on the symptom. Whilst this may, in the short term, exacerbate the problem, it can often change it very significantly, especially once the additional fear and emotion that might be raised by this exercise are expressed.[24] By working directly with the symptom in the transpersonal counselling mode with a nurse or counsellor, the symptoms can be given meaning and perhaps a colour, shape or voice, and it is often surprising how bringing consciousness to symptoms in this way can transform or improve them, and often provide extremely relevant, meaningful insight at the same time.

In attempting to transcend symptoms, one does exactly the reverse. Here the mind is used to distract you from the symptom through alternative stimulation, such as music, or involvement with creative activity, humour, excursions into nature or to the theatre or cinema, or through involvement in other meaningful activity or meditation. The techniques of visualization or self-hypnosis can also be used; here, a new focus is found for the mind so that the mind's focus is taken away from the stimulus of the symptom. These techniques are particularly useful in the management of chronic pain and nausea.

## Complementary therapies for symptom relief
The following list gives an idea of which therapies are especially useful in the relief of specific symptoms:

### Anxiety or insomnia
Aromatherapy, breathing techniques, yoga, t'ai chi, gentle exercise, counselling, homoeopathic and herbal remedies.

**Pain**
Breathing exercises, mental focus, mental transcendence, acupuncture, reflexology, music therapy.

**Fatigue and loss of motivation**
Spiritual healing, the energy medicines of acupuncture, shiatsu, homoeopathy.

**Nausea**
Sea-bands applied to the P6 acupuncture point at the wrist, acupuncture, homoeopathic remedies, root ginger, slippery elm, imagery.

**Constipation**
Reflexology, psyllium husks, slippery elm or senna, colonic irrigation (if severe or prolonged).

**Diarrhoea**
Psyllium husks, acupuncture or reflexology.

**Breathlessness**
Acupuncture, relaxation, yogic breathing techniques.

**Weight loss**
Wholefood build-up drinks made from soya protein (tofu), mixed with soya milk, plus bananas or avocados, and other flavourings as appropriate, taken regularly between meals.

**Appetite loss**
Acupuncture, reflexology, homoeopathy, herbal medicine.

**Chemotherapy side-effects**
As for nausea (*see* above), plus aloe vera juice or slippery elm (for gastro-intestinal epithelial damage), chamomile mouthwash and zinc pastilles (for a sore mouth), and kelp (for strengthening

hair and nails). Visualization aids the ability to cope mentally with chemotherapy, and it has also been demonstrated to improve nausea symptoms, immune function and prognosis in breast cancer patients.[8] Relaxation therapy is also associated with less distress, less nausea, and lower arousal following chemotherapy.[25] Sidergren et al (1994) found that touch and relaxation in combination were the most effective at reducing symptoms of distress and severity of symptoms before and after chemotherapy.[26]

## Radiotherapy side-effects

Aromatherapy cream (containing vitamin E and skin-soothing oils to prevent skin burning).[27] Homoeopathic and flower remedies (to combat fatigue, dizziness or nausea caused by radiotherapy).[28] Visualization techniques can help replace negative associations with more positive healing images of radiotherapy.

# Are Orthodox Cancer Medicine and the Holistic Approach Really Compatible?

Purists will argue that it is nonsense to see the orthodox medical approach as compatible with holistic medicine. They say that these two approaches are diametrically opposed because the holistic approach is aimed at protecting and strengthening tissue functioning whilst chemotherapy and radiotherapy are destructive to newly growing tissue, including the immune system. In fact, many go further, pointing out that chemotherapy and radiotherapy are themselves carcinogenic, and that common treatments such as Tamoxifen carry many side-effects, including an increased risk of cancer of the uterus (which is seldom mentioned).

For these reasons increasing numbers of people opt for alternative or holistic approaches alone, altogether stepping outside of the medical process and any support this may have given them. This is a very tough path: many have trodden it with resounding success, but others have been unsuccessful; and currently it is impossible to know which of the alternative treatments will produce what results for which people. Many people faced with these agonizing choices feel morally obliged to have all treatments on offer, conventional and complementary, mainly for the sake of their families (especially if there are small children to consider).

The positive view of combining holistic and orthodox therapies is that holistic medicine can provide support to the system to help combat the down side of conventional interventions, most especially in helping to repair damage to healthy tissue straight away.

Many protagonists of alternative therapies insist that people will have far better outcomes if they use natural medicines alone, and they find the metabolic clinics in Europe and Mexico the most useful option. However, this view places the individual with cancer under acute pressure to decide 'which camp to join'. The decision to use one therapy in preference to another must be thought about carefully and decided on an absolutely individual basis. In cases in which the cancer is low grade and in its early stages the individual has time on their side, and can therefore opt to work with alternative approaches alone for a period and then judge for themselves whether or not they are achieving stabilization or regression of their disease.

In other situations there may be a time imperative – in cases where there is a possibility of a tumour's becoming inoperable, for example, or posing a threat locally to nervous or arterial tissue. In such cases, urgent medical intervention may be required as a life-saving procedure or to prevent disability. It may also be advisable to remove a tumour if there is a risk that it will break through the skin and develop into a nasty, ulcerating lesion. The best course of action for those faced with this dilemma is, again, to talk to an holistic doctor, who will help you to evaluate realistically which option or combination of options would be best for you when all the various factors and personal views are taken into consideration. In this way, it is hoped that you will be able to decide on a course of action that both honours your personal needs and keeps you as safe as possible.

# PART THREE

# THE BRISTOL
# EXPERIENCE

# 9

# The Bristol Cancer
# Help Centre

The Cancer Help Centre's *raison d'être* is quite simply to offer healing and support both to people with any form of cancer and to those who support them. The Centre's approach is holistic in the sense that it recognizes the unity and interdependence of body, mind and spirit within each individual. The Centre seeks first, through the teaching of the holistic approach to health, and then by implementation of the holistic medical model, to help individuals achieve the optimum level of health for the remainder of their lives, however long or short that may be.

The primary focus of the work at the Centre is the therapy services, but in addition to these the Centre has developed extensive educational, informational and research services, and these are available to people with cancer, their supporters, healthcare professionals, and the general public.

## The Centre's Services

Since the Bristol Approach necessitates commitment to healthy lifestyle changes, rather than simply to a treatment programme, it is important to ensure that people come to the Centre with the right expectations. To help you determine whether the Bristol Approach is likely to be right for you, it is recommended that you send for the introductory pack, which includes an audio tape about the services of the Centre, and a video tape giving a full explanation of the holistic model, and the philosophy, theory, science and practice underpinning the Bristol Approach.

In summary, the services of the Bristol Cancer Help Centre are:

- Booking service.
- Telephone helpline, including counselling and advice.
- Bristol Cancer Help Centre website.
- Shop and mail-order service.
- Therapy programme.
- Doctor phone-in.
- Help with death and dying.
- Bristol support group.
- Regional support centres.
- National and international therapeutic and support network.
- Library and information service.
- Consultancy services.
- Education and research services.

## Booking service

All bookings are taken by the Centre's booking assistant, who is dedicated to organizing swift and efficient access to the Centre. In cases of financial hardship the assistant will endeavour to help individuals obtain bursary funding.

## Telephone helpline

At any time during the year, clients of the Centre can receive counselling or advice by telephoning the Centre's helpline. Arrangements can be made for callers to speak to specific therapists, the catering consultant, or the doctor, as appropriate. And it is also possible to come to the Centre for one-to-one appointments with a counsellor, healer or doctor.

The helpline is staffed by understanding people who will comfort and advise those with cancer and their supporters when they are in distress. They will give sympathy, encouragement and hope, as well as information about the holistic approach to health and how to obtain access to the Centre's services. Any callers that are unable to enrol on the Centre's therapy programme will be told how to find holistic facilities in their own area. The helpline staff will also supply useful information about other kinds of cancer support agency.

Callers who think they may be interested in using the services of the Bristol Cancer Help Centre are advised to order the Centre's introductory pack (*see* pages 133–4). The helpline is accessed through the reception desk at the Bristol Cancer Help Centre, on 0117 980 9500 or directly on 0117 980 9505.

## Bristol Cancer Help Centre website
The Bristol Cancer Help Centre has a website, which contains information on all aspects of the Centre and its work. The address of the website is: http://www.bristolcancerhelp.org

## Shop and mail-order service
The Centre's shop supplies a wealth of books, video and audio tapes, herbal remedies, and vitamin and mineral supplements. Between 1.00 p.m and 6.00 p.m there is an assistant present to deal with customers in person, and to take telephone orders (0117 980 9504). A comprehensive mail-order form is included in the Centre's introductory pack (*see* pages 133–4). The shop can also be accessed via the Centre's website (*see* above).

## Therapy programme
Details of the Centre's therapy programme are given in the introductory pack. To obtain maximum benefit, people with cancer, and their supporters, are in the first instance encouraged to embark upon a year's programme with the Centre. This involves a two-day introductory course, a five-day residential course, and two follow-up visits throughout the year, with nurse follow-up (*see* page 149) between each visit.

## Doctor phone-in

Once a week there is an holistic doctor available for telephone consultations at the Centre.

Appointments to speak to the doctor can be booked in advance through reception. This enables you to gain remote access to an holistic doctor who will be able to advise you on any new medical problems that you may have developed, and, where necessary, to support you through the process of making decisions.

## Help with death and dying

The Bristol Cancer Help Centre has members of staff who specialize in helping clients who wish to consciously explore their feelings about death or their actual dying process. Help can be arranged by phoning the Centre reception or helpline.

## Bristol support group

The Centre has its own support group (based at the Centre's premises) for those in the south and west regions of the UK.

## Regional support centres

In the UK, there are approximately 30 holistic cancer support groups that are based directly along Bristol lines. (*See* Appendix II.) There are others around the world, too, which have been established by people who have been to Bristol either as students or clients. All the Centre's clients are given a list of these 'affiliated' support groups.

## National and international therapeutic and support network

The Centre has an extensive network of contacts, throughout Britain and abroad, with organizations and support groups that are able to provide details of local practitioners and offer ongoing support for those who have embarked upon the Bristol Approach. Many of these are listed in Appendix II.

## Library and information service

The Centre has an excellent library of books, journals and tapes for use by clients staying at the Centre. It holds information on the full spectrum of complementary and alternative holistic approaches to cancer, and written requests for information are answered by the Centre's librarian/information officer (with assistance where necessary from the Centre's doctors).

The Centre also holds databases of scientific reference material on cancer and nutrition, cancer and the mind, and cancer and the environment.

## Consultancy services

The Centre's therapy director, holistic medical consultant and therapists are available to give consultative advice to those wishing to set up national and/or international holistic support services for people with cancer.

## Education and research services

The Centre has an extensive education department offering in-house and university-accredited courses in the holistic approach to health and cancer. Talks and lectures by Centre staff are given both nationally and internationally, and the Centre regularly hosts major international speakers who are at the cutting edge of the holistic approach. Research and audit are carried out at the Centre by the therapy and education departments.

# Usership of the Centre

Approximately 1,000 people come on the Centre's programmes each year, most of whom come at the point of secondary diagnosis. Many of them come with their supporters. Since 1998 it has been the Centre's policy to offer specific places to supporters rather than accommodating them purely in their role as escort. This move has been made in recognition of the intense stress, distress and vulnerability associated with their role.

The ratio of women with cancer to men with cancer who use the Centre is around 3 to 1, but this is balanced somewhat by the presence of rather more male supporters. This gender difference is reflected generally throughout the holistic therapy and self-help areas of medicine. Since breast cancer is the most common female cancer, we see a lot of women with breast cancer at Bristol, but over the last 20 years the staff at the Centre have had the opportunity to help people with every type of cancer. It is hoped that over time, as education and information about the Bristol Approach spreads, more men with cancer will use the Centre, and that more people will come upon receiving primary diagnosis.

Around 50 per cent of the Centre's clients come from the London area, 25 per cent from the south and west of England, and about 20 per cent from the remaining parts of the British Isles; about 5 per cent come from outside the UK. Since its early days Bristol has attracted significant numbers of people from other countries because it always has been and remains almost unique in offering its residential mind–body–spirit programme. People from all classes and backgrounds use the Centre, and pains are taken to ensure that those that are committed to using the Centre's approach are not barred from access on financial grounds.

## The Centre's Management and Funding

The Bristol Cancer Help Centre is a charity run by a board of trustees. The day-to-day management is undertaken by the Centre's chief executive, who is supported by around 20 staff, plus volunteers, who help with fund-raising and administration. Each year the fund-raising department has to raise half a million pounds over and above the fees from the therapy and education services in order to ensure the viability of the Centre. The Centre is therefore entirely dependent on the generosity and support of its long-term donors and the Friends of The Bristol Cancer Help Centre.

# 10

# *The Bristol Programme*

Getting started on the Bristol programme quite simply involves sending for the introductory pack and booking on to the first part of the programme, which is the introductory course (*see* Chapter 9).

It is helpful to begin the recommended vitamin and mineral regime as soon as you can, rather than waiting until you come to Bristol (*see* page 94). It is also a good idea to start addressing the question of changing your diet. To this end you will be helped by reading *Healing Foods*, by Dr Rosy Daniel and *The Healing Foods Cookbook*, written by the Centre's catering consultant, Jane Sen (*see* Further Reading)

The therapy programme at Bristol has been designed to take account of the many levels at which the healing process is initiated, and also to give you sufficient time both to make the necessary life changes and to re-enforce them, so that you are able to receive maximum benefit from the programme. The course therefore runs over a year, which might at first seem a long time, and a big commitment for you to make. But this is brought into perspective when you consider that embarking on the course can be a vital first step in the process of learning to invest properly in your own health and development, and as a result, to enhance your overall well-being and happiness.

The Bristol programme is designed for people with cancer and, equally, for those who support them closely. This is because Bristol recognizes that the diagnosis of cancer in a loved one is just as much a life-changing event for the supporter as it is for the person with cancer. (*See* Chapter 7.) Therefore all the following descriptions of the courses and their aims apply equally to both people with cancer and their supporters.

# The Therapeutic Aims of the Bristol Programme

In overview, the therapeutic aims of the Bristol Cancer Help Centre programme can be divided into three phases:

## *Phase I*

- Promote recovery from the shock of diagnosis of cancer: this involves 'the telling of your story' and being properly heard by the therapeutic team.
- Elicit your needs and expectations, naming fears and anxieties.
- Appraisal, examination and evaluation of the state of your health, both by you and the professional holistic therapeutic team.
- Explain the range of orthodox, complementary and alternative medical options.
- Provide counselling to help with medical decision-making processes, help with symptom control from the cancer and the side-effects of its treatment, and individualized advice regarding supplements.
- Restore a sense of hope, and establish a belief in your power to affect your own quality of life and health.
- Help in establishing a personalized therapeutic and self-help plan.
- Help with symptom control and the side-effects of cancer treatment.
- Reduce fear, isolation and anxiety.
- Achieve shift in attitude to *living with* cancer, rather than *dying from* cancer.

- Lift energy levels through spiritual healing to achieve a pronounced improvement in your ability to cope and to become involved in a self-help programme.
- Provide specific support through cancer treatment, and help with adjustment to loss, physical and emotional, and throughout the grieving process this creates.
- Maximize the efficacy, and reduce the side-effects, of conventional treatment by:
  (a) ensuring genuinely informed, active choice and willing participation in all treatments, medical and complementary;
  (b) fostering a sense of control;
  (c) reducing fear levels;
  (d) achieving relaxation; and
  (e) developing positive feelings and images around your medical treatment.
- Help the family and carers to deal with their grief, anxiety, stress, and other needs.

## Phase II
- Formulate your therapeutic plan to improve health, energy and prognosis.
- Help with the formation of your self-help plan to improve health, energy and prognosis.
- Help with the formation of a personalized nutrition plan.
- Encourage the development of a support network.
- Encourage the establishment of a personal therapy team.
- Examine personal lifestyle, attitudes and stress (external and self-stressing), to support you through making the necessary changes to become happier and less stressed.
- Introduce the role of the mind in affecting the physiology of the body and future life and illness outcomes.
- Explore personal core values, meaning and purpose in life.
- Explore personal goals, dreams and ambitions, and provide encouragement and support to enable you to achieve these.
- Help in the regaining of a strong sense of 'Self'.

- Promote happiness, well-being, enthusiasm and commitment to life.
- Develop a personal spirituality and sources of spiritual nourishment.
- Help in enabling you to become 'true to yourself' and to become authentic in the day-to-day life choices you make.
- Help in establishing a healthy nutritional/eating pattern that is optimally healthy and personally tailored to your need.
- Encourage personal creativity and use of creative therapies to help with healing, and to help you rediscover your sense of play, fun and self-expression.

## Phase III

- Help in enabling you to look more deeply into the nature of life, and at what feeds and nourishes, or drains and depletes you.
- Help in refining your own lifestyle and personal practices to achieve optimum health.
- Help in looking more closely at your fears, beliefs and relationship to death, in order that you may become less fearful of death and even go on to prepare consciously for dying, if that becomes appropriate.
- Help in achieving a 'personal transformation' that enables you to use the illness as an opportunity for deepening your self-awareness and enhancing your development and growth: helping you to find new meaning, value and purpose in life – coming to live very contentedly in the present.

# The Therapy Programme

The therapy programme is ongoing and regularly reviewed. Currently it runs over a year and includes:

- The introductory pack.
- The introductory course.

- The residential course.
- Two follow-up days.
- Nurse follow-up by phone.

## The introductory pack

The introductory pack is designed to give you an overall idea of what the Bristol programme is, and how it might meet your individual needs, so that you can decide whether the programme is suitable for you. The contents of the introductory pack are described in Chapter 9.

## The introductory course

Before attending the introductory course you are asked to begin the process of self-evaluation by completing a self-assessment form. This will help you to start thinking about what the key questions and issues are for you so that you can make the very best use of the time you have with the therapy team at Bristol.

The introductory course is residential and lasts for two days. It is very much about meeting others with similar problems, starting the process of recovery from diagnosis, and starting to learn and experience the self-help techniques. On day two, you meet members of the therapy team one-to-one and have in-depth sessions to individualize your assessment and therapy planning process. There will be appointments with the holistic doctor, counsellor, nutritional therapist, and art therapist. By the end of the two days you will have a very clear picture about your therapeutic and self-help needs and will be well and truly embarked on your holistic self-healing journey.

The overall objectives of the introductory course are included in the list of aims in Phase I. One of the great benefits of embarking on this initial course is that it enables you to experience solidarity and closeness with others who are going through similar experiences. This plays an important part in helping to achieve many of the course's aims, most especially in reducing the sense of isolation that many people feel after diagnosis. And for the many people who find the idea of making drastic changes in diet quite challenging, the residential introductory course is especially helpful in that it provides the opportunity for you to discover how delicious good healthy food can be. You will be introduced to organic, vegan food, and experience the style of eating to be aimed for at home.

## The residential course

The residential course is a five-day course designed to deepen the therapeutic process that you will have begun on the two-day introductory course. Having obtained a very clear picture from the two-day course about the state of your lifestyle, spirit, emotions and energy, the residential week provides you with the most superb opportunity to look more deeply at the big questions of what motivation and underlying beliefs are directing you and your life. It is literally the chance to 'stop the world and get off' for a week, so that you can let go of all your normal considerations – even forgetting that the cancer exists, if that seems possible – in order to get down to the important questions of who you are, and what really matters to you in life.

Some of the questions that the residential course will encourage you to ask are:

- Where do I wish to put my precious life energy in order to experience the most fulfilment and joy in my life?
- What are my beliefs about living and dying?
- What fears are choking my life energy, and how can I release these fears?

Whilst this process is going on, your energy will simultaneously be lifted through healing, counselling, massage, shiatsu, meditation, visualization, and relaxation. You will also receive advice on your diet and your individual nutritional needs, and there is skilled group facilitation by counsellors, music therapists, and holistic nurses.

The main objectives of the residential week-long course are outlined in Phases II and III on pages 141–2. Primarily it is about receiving spiritual healing and uplift, and taking the time to rest and recover from life's pressures and the difficulties of illness and its treatment so that you can explore your core values, establish your reason for living, and regain sight of what is important in life. Through this process you can establish your commitment to life or, if appropriate, give yourself permission to let go into your dying process. As you explore yourself and the issues that are relevant to you, you will continue to receive on-going guidance, support and therapy from doctors, nurses and body therapists, and be encouraged to formulate your own self-help plans that will support and stimulate your healing and recovery.

Through learning the skills of personal imagery and affirmation, you will increase your understanding of the role of the mind in affecting the physiology of the body, and future life and illness outcomes. You will continue to learn the self-help techniques of meditation, visualization and relaxation, and to form a healthy eating plan, strengthening your body through excellent food, exercise, stretching and breathwork. In doing this you will increase your awareness of the body's energy state, and learn the skills to improve this on a day-to-day basis.

The residential course can be an intense experience in that it provides you with the support that enables you to journey into your pain, to express intense and difficult emotions, to face your fear, losses, disability, despair and anger and, if desired, to face death itself. This chance to air the unspeakable often liberates a great deal of trapped energy, which can lead to an enormous sense of relief and renewed vitality.

Through these processes you will be able to focus on the positive side of your experience of illness, enabling you to:

• Work through and resolve the negative emotions and situations that block your life and healing.

- Look at the possible secondary gains of the illness, and learn how to get the same benefits in healthy ways.
- Look at the message the cancer may be giving you.
- Experience creativity and self-expression through art, music and movement.
- Become 'true to yourself' by becoming more aware of your feelings.
- Become bolder and clearer in communicating your needs to others (for some people this may involve assertiveness training) and more authentic in the way you make your day-to-day and life choices.

## Residential week outcomes

I have lost count of the number of people who have said to me that the residential week at the Bristol Cancer Help Centre was the best week of their lives. Indeed, many have said that everyone should go through this programme – regardless of whether or not they have cancer – so that they can look at how they are living, shed their fears, and learn to express themselves and their potential fully.

The changes people go through during the residential week range from being very practical and outwardly focused to very profound and more to do with the inner state of being. Whichever they are, people almost always leave the residential week deeply heartened by the experience and the loving support and encouragement they have felt during their visit.

The extremely potent atmosphere that exists during this week is created through the mutual bonding of the members of the group who attend, and the highly individualized care given by the multi-disciplinary team of holistic therapists who meet three times a day to give each other constant feedback on the evolving needs and state of all participants as the week's process unfolds. Of course the most basic ingredients are a combination of the Centre's healing environment (which feels safe enough for individuals to embark upon a deep self-healing journey) and

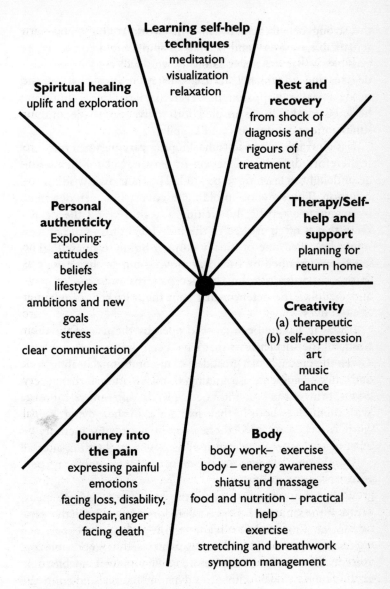

**Learning self-help techniques**
meditation
visualization
relaxation

**Rest and recovery**
from shock of diagnosis and rigours of treatment

**Spiritual healing**
uplift and exploration

**Therapy/Self-help and support**
planning for return home

**Personal authenticity**
Exploring:
attitudes
beliefs
lifestyles
ambitions and new goals
stress
clear communication

**Creativity**
(a) therapeutic
(b) self-expression
art
music
dance

**Journey into the pain**
expressing painful emotions
facing loss, disability, despair, anger
facing death

**Body**
body work– exercise
body – energy awareness
shiatsu and massage
food and nutrition – practical help
exercise
stretching and breathwork
symptom management

*Model for the components of the residential week.*

the strong belief (held by all who work at the centre) that remarkable recovery and healing of spirit, mind and body are possible. What we never know is who will recover, to what degree, and at which level the greatest healing changes will occur. It is always apparent however, that if the spirit is lifted and healed the individual is enabled both to live, and to die, immeasurably more comfortably and happily.

It is clear that the road to healing is a very personal one, and it therefore differs from person to person, but for all there is great delight in learning to be guided by their own wisdom and intuition. This sense of unfolding discovery has been described by many as a terrifically exciting adventure, and the deeper sense that is often created in the individual during the process might be called one of 'finally coming home to oneself'. This has been described by others as moving out of their false self, in other words discarding learned patterns and ways of being and shedding the defences that kept them locked in unhappy, limited lives.

It is as if, having been cracked open by the fear of the diagnosis, all the smaller fears that have been limiting life implode. Given the presence of a great deal of unconditional healing, love and encouragement, astounding transformational change can occur, bringing people into a completely different relationship with themselves both in their living and in their dying. As the spirit is healed or lifted there is often a growing memory or awareness that in fact death itself is not so frightening after all and, as this process deepens, the sense of inner strength and personal authority grows.

With this growing awareness, the resistance to change melts, whilst at the same time there is a paradoxical increase in the sense of control. This might be likened to the feeling you experience when you first succeed at riding a bicycle. As impossible and improbable as it felt the day before when you were unable to do it, you are now able to hold this dynamic balance and enjoy the great new freedom that it gives you.

## *The follow-up day*

The follow-up day is a one-day course that can be undertaken at any time after attending the week-long residential course.

It is highly recommended that at least two follow-up days are attended during the first year in order to consolidate the work done on the residential course. The day starts with a group, first to relax and then to share together the thrills and spills of life and the healing process since the last visit to Bristol. One of the great pleasures of this day is that newcomers meet the inspiring people who have been coming to Bristol for years and will witness the marvellous example that they set: as many of these people say, 'I should have been dead years ago.'

This introductory group is followed by one-to-one sessions with the doctor, healer, nutritional therapist and counsellor, and the art room is available all day for creative self-expression. After lunch there is a long meditation to re-enforce the learning of meditation skills, and at the end of the day there is another discussion forum to reflect on the progress made and to trouble-shoot any outstanding problems. The day finishes with an empowering visualization to send you on your way.

## *The follow-up nurse*

It must be acknowledged that the process that Bristol is offering to its clients is a complex and demanding one. Essentially, it involves the taking on board of a new model of healthcare before starting, and choosing between and embarking upon many new practices and therapies.

In order to maintain the programme that you have created through your visits to Bristol, it is very important that in the early stages help and support are available to help you make the right contacts in the home environment. To this end the follow-up nurse will phone clients between courses at Bristol to give the necessary guidance and encouragement, and generally hear how things are going. This feedback enables Bristol to determine the  extent to which people continue to implement the

---

**The aims of the follow-up day**

The aims of the follow-up day are to help you to:

- Define your current needs and expectations, naming and talking about fears and anxieties.
- Reassess your state of mind, body and spirit, and adjust your self-help and therapy plan accordingly.
- Receive medical counselling to help you consider any new medical developments or symptoms, and to assist you in your decision-making processes.
- Re-establish your belief in your own power to affect your own well-being, quality of life and health.
- Continue to make the changes in your lifestyle and personal attitudes to achieve optimum health.
- Continue to enhance your enthusiasm and commitment to yourself – rekindling your dedication to life or, if appropriate, helping you to let go.

---

Bristol programme once they get back home and are subjected to their old pressures and the expectations of others; in addition it provides Bristol with valuable information about the quality of the courses and the clients' reaction to them.

## The Therapists and Therapies at the Bristol Cancer Help Centre

*The holistic doctor*
The holistic doctor provides a bridge between the worlds of orthodox and holistic medicine, supporting you in the process of taking charge of your situation, and working step-by-step towards the recovery of health. The holistic doctor is also there

to help in the initial evaluation of the state of mind, body and spirit, as well as the process of sorting out what the therapeutic and self-help plan should be according to your needs at the time of consultation. This will involve helping you to choose the right alternative and complementary medicines.

The holistic doctor can also help you take time to understand your illness or its treatment, and to assess the medical options you are being given, counselling you through the process of making truly informed decisions about the treatments you are being offered. The doctor can advise on the tailoring of nutritional approaches to your specific medical conditions and fine-tune your nutritional supplementation regime of vitamins and minerals and other natural medicines.

## The holistic nurse

Holistic nurses are trained to provide care and support, and to help with symptom control with natural medicines, massage and self-help techniques.

Often, a holistic nurse will be able to help control symptoms by reducing fear levels through visualization, relaxation, breathing techniques and comforting support, and further improvement can be gained through the use of natural remedies drawn from the spectrum of herbal medicine, homoeopathy and Bach Flower Remedies. Some holistic nurses are also trained in therapeutic touch, which is a form of healing designed to help soothe and calm the system, and thus to reduce symptoms.

## The holistic counsellor and group therapist

Because of the relationship between mind and body, counselling is an absolutely pivotal part of the holistic healing process, and some of the most successful mind–body counselling is done by counsellors that are trained in the transpersonal or psychosynthesis schools.

In dealing with serious illnesses the first thing that is most often needed from the counsellor is support to grieve for the loss of your 'normal' situation and to adjust to the new reality that is facing you. Once through this part of the process it is important to continue seeing a counsellor to work out how the crisis of illness can be transformed into the opportunity for much deeper healing.

## The benefits of the Bristol Approach

Over 20 years, observation of the Bristol Approach indicates that receiving loving support and embracing the holistic approach can bring extremely positive benefits to physical, emotional and spiritual well-being, by:

- Reducing fear – achieving a calm, balanced, happy state of mind through healing massage, relaxation and counselling.
- Strengthening the body – through stress reduction, healthy eating, vitamin and mineral supplementation, and physical exercise such as yoga, t'ai chi and chi gong.
- Raising your energy – through spiritual healing, shiatsu and creative self-expression.
- Healing the heart – by letting go of past hurts and disappointment, and by learning to express emotion, improve communication and become true to yourself.
- Changing your mind – replacing limiting or unhealthy attitudes or beliefs with very strongly life-affirming messages, images and goals.
- Lifting the spirit – by focusing on what gives you joy, fulfilment, purpose and meaning in your life.
- Enhancing your life – building a healthy, fulfilling lifestyle around your newly prioritized values and sources of nourishment.

This type of counselling includes the spiritual and creative or 'right-brain' aspects of the mind, which 'think' in images and symbols, and which communicate with us through our dreams and inner visual or imagination processes. By working with this part of the mind it is often possible to access very quickly the emotional truth of what is going on as we learn to listen to the inner voice and inherent wisdom of our 'higher self', 'wise observer' or simply the intuitive, knowing aspect of ourselves. This inner wisdom is often very under-used in our normal busy left-brain dominated way of being, and it is especially helpful in crisis to be able to access this part of ourselves so that we can make the decisions that are truly congruent with our innermost sense of what is right for us and what will help us begin to be well again.

Most people think that counselling is about the relief of emotional distress only, but transpersonal counselling is very much about helping us to see again what aspects of ourselves are right and strong, as well as helping us to re-identify with our true nature and more authentic sense of self. The counsellor can act as a mirror, helping us to see what we know to be true about ourselves, particularly seeing the patterns or ties, or counter-productive situations that need releasing, so that our life and energies will start to flow freely again.

Through this counselling, what we know and feel can be revealed and connected with very quickly, and we can be helped to identify what our soul and spirit are yearning for, which may even be to let go and die. Although on the surface we may seem to be actively fighting illness, at a deeper level we may have made quite a different choice; and, by connecting to our deeper reality through counselling, great truth and peace can be established.

In counselling we can look at our feelings about death and dying, and once these fears have been confronted we can often feel an enormous new lease of life as the fear of death (which may have been affecting us for many years) dissipates. Conversely we may be yearning quite literally to come back to life, and rediscover our passion and potential as we take new directions, or fulfil our most important needs and ambitions.

We can also look at our relationships, and particularly examine the way we may be stuck or losing tremendous amounts of energy by repeating the same unsatisfactory relationship patterns over and over again. And we can look at our 'sub-personalities', of which there may be many. Often there may be a bossy, dominant or highly critical sub-personality, which is overshadowing a gentler, more creative aspect of ourselves; or an over-serious, over-responsible part that is overshadowing a playful, creative or humorous aspect of ourselves. In this way we get to know who is running the show in our lives, and we can begin, as our awareness develops, to change the balance.

## Group therapy

Getting to know and understand ourselves better can take place during group therapy. It is extremely helpful to meet with people who have the same problems or needs as ourselves. The sense of identification, support and solidarity that can be engendered during group therapy provides many people with an enormous sense of relief from the isolation and alienation that they feel, especially when they have an extremely serious illness.

Surprisingly, it can be easier to let go and express your emotions with the support of the group than it is with friends or family, or even in a one-to-one session with a therapist or counsellor. It can also be very constructive to work together to identify needs and common underlying beliefs and patterns, which may be sabotaging different members of the group. With the mutual support and encouragement provided by members of the group, individuals can often feel bold enough to express creative ideas about new values and priorities, as well as learning self-help techniques together.

This type of group therapy is facilitated by a professional group psychotherapist, but there are support groups that are more social in nature and that can also be extremely helpful in continuing support and resource sharing, as well as in receiving and giving practical help with any problems that may arise.

## Creative therapies

The creative therapies used at the Bristol Cancer Help Centre are music, movement and art. These can be extremely freeing, allowing people to express what they may find difficult to put into words. They require no previous skill or expertise, and can often be linked very successfully with group therapeutic work, deepening the experience and giving an outlet for what arises through visualization processes or individual psychotherapeutic work.

Creative therapies can also rejuvenate the more playful, joyful, creative aspect of our natures, enabling us to capture again the feeling of energy and fun that we took for granted in youth.

## Spiritual healing

Spiritual healing, or the 'laying on of hands', has its roots in the Christian tradition and was historically as important a part of Christ's ministry as his teaching.

Spiritual healers channel pure loving energy from a higher energy source, which is perceived by the healer either as being divine, i.e., from God, Christ or angelic sources, or (if the healer is working from the Reiki or more general, atheist perspective) from the life force of the planet. From the recipient's point of view the healing is non-denominational and is beyond any personal religion or belief system. It is a completely natural, universal connection with the spiritual quality of each person.

> I was very wary when I had my first healing experience. I didn't know what to expect. But I went in open-minded, and I was very nicely surprised. It was this feeling of calmness and peacefulness that I felt instantly. I continued having healing over a long period of time, about once a week

155

for two years. It was always this feeling of stillness – it was a very positive experience. It helped me to be empowered really – to continue with the fighting spirit and to get well again.

*Jenny Jackson: living with liver cancer,*
*first diagnosed in 1987*

Healers are able to sense where the energy is low in the individual, and to allow their hands to stay by this empty place until the energy has stopped flowing from them. They then move until they sense another place where the energy begins to flow. As such it is not they themselves that are doing the healing; rather it is that they sense where the energy is required and allow the process to happen. This has the remarkable effect of raising the energy levels greatly whilst simultaneously calming and lifting the spirit.

Whilst healers themselves have their own specific belief systems, they are discouraged through their code of ethics to share these belief systems with their clients, aiming to keep the healing environment as neutral as possible. However, where people do have strong religious beliefs it is possible to find a healer who is of their own spiritual denomination, and this can provide a very safe and reinforcing environment for the individual's spiritual belief and practice.

## The energy medicines

Energy medicines can play a crucial role in the rebalancing and recharging of your system. The most well-known classical systems are acupuncture, shiatsu, homoeopathy and ayurvedic medicine, which all work to balance and restore the flow of the vital energy in the body.

### Shiatsu

Shiatsu is a form of acupressure that originated in Japan. It combines healing touch with subtle energy rebalancing.

**Acupuncture**

Acupuncture originates from China. The acupuncture therapist uses very fine needles to rebalance the energy flow in the body's meridians.

**Homoeopathy**

The principle of homoeopathy, which has its origins in Europe, is that 'like cures like'. This means that the symptoms that a particular substance produces can be cured by that same substance if it is given in homoeopathic doses. Homoeopathic medicines support the person's underlying constitution, strengthening their 'vital force' and ability to combat disease. They are given in the form of tiny pills, which are prescribed after very detailed and precise consultation with a homoeopath or holistic doctor.

**Ayurvedic medicine**

Ayurvedic medicine, which is based on ancient Indian medicine and yogic practice, uses a combination of diet, herbs, massage and yoga to bring the system back into balance.

---

**Monitoring progress with energy medicines**

The therapist using the energy medicines is able to diagnose the state of your 'vital energy', giving you valuable feedback that will enable you, over the weeks and months of using these medicines, to find out what effect your self-help efforts and life-style changes are having.

---

*Body work*

Body work with massage, aromatherapy or reflexology (which is a form of acupressure to the feet), can be useful and reassuring, especially if illness has caused you to feel alienated from your body. When this happens, the loving touch of a body therapist can help you get past the hurt or alienation felt as a result of illness or its treatment. Contrary to popular belief, massage is not contraindicated in cancer.

These therapies can also put you into a deep state of relaxation which will boost symptom reduction and assist deeper healing, since improvement in mind–body states leads to improvement in immune function.

## Nutritional therapy

There are many nutritional therapeutic approaches to illness, where food itself is being used as the medicine. The best known of these are naturopathy, macrobiotics, fasting, juice diets and, in the cancer world, the Gerson diet.

These approaches work because they are all based on feeding the body with extremely high-quality nutrition that has been specifically tailored to the body's type and condition. Bristol will support individuals who wish to embark upon these nutritional therapies whole-heartedly, but they are often very rigorous and demand great application. Many people prefer to adopt a more long-term, healthy eating approach, and this is now the policy of Bristol Cancer Help Centre.

The healthy eating approach used at the Bristol Cancer Help Centre stresses the importance of making sure that you eat vegetables and fruit, preferably organic, with every meal. To ensure that they retain as much of their goodness as possible, these foods should be served either raw in salads, or lightly stir-fried or steamed. It is also very important to eat food that is not processed or that contains food additives, and to go, where possible, for the wholefood or 'brown' option (brown rice, brown bread and brown flour, and so on).

At the same time, all efforts must be made to decrease the animal food consumed in the diet, particularly the amount of animal fat. In addition to this, sugar, salt and protein intake should be reduced, as should the consumption of stimulants such as coffee, tea and excessive alcohol.

When I came on the course at Bristol I realized very quickly how important the diet was. It was surprisingly easy for
me to make the change to being a vegan. It also felt like a
very positive thing to do. I went home and gave up certain
foods, which weren't doing me any good, made the
changes, and very quickly afterwards I started feeling a lot
better – mentally, because it was good actually doing something constructive and, physically, because my energy got
better. So overall it was a very profound thing for me to do.

*Jenny Jackson: living with liver cancer,*
*first diagnosed in 1987*

The problem in the West is that we are simultaneously overfed
and under-nourished: this is because we eat very high-calorie
foods, full of fat and sugar, but lack sufficient vitamins, minerals, and the vital plant chemicals that we need to stay healthy and
protected from heart disease and cancer.

One of the keys to changing diet successfully is to add the extra
fruit, vegetables and juices before taking other things away, so
that the change-over is gradual and there is no feeling of depri-
vation. When people first start to eat well, they may experience
some weight loss, but this should stabilize as the healthy diet
becomes established. The important thing here is not to forget to
eat enough carbohydrates and vegetable oils (in the form of pasta,
grains and bread, olive and linseed oils), especially if weight loss
is already a problem. Some people can become so focused on the
raw vegetable and juice components of their new diet that they
omit to eat enough 'energy foods' and calories.

If possible, start growing your own food. Even if you do not
have a vegetable garden, it is worth growing herbs or sprouts in
the kitchen or on the windowsill, or even intermingling vegetables with flowers in hanging baskets and flowerbeds.

If you are worried at all about changes in your body as a result
of changing diet, you should immediately consult an holistic
doctor or nutritionist.

**Recommended supplements**

Bristol Cancer Help Centre recommends the anti-oxidant vitamins and minerals A, C and E, zinc and selenium, and vitamin B complete. Vitamin A is given as its safe precursor, beta-carotene, in its natural form. This regime is often supplemented with Co-enzyme Q 10 and aerobic oxygen to help energize the intra-cellular respiratory/energy producing mechanisms. Dosage instructions are given in the introductory pack and on page 94.

## Herbal medicine

Help can be gained from the world of herbal medicine, either European or Oriental. Here traditional remedies are chosen for their role in aiding specific conditions and symptoms. They can provide effective help particularly in cleansing the body and strengthening the tissues, and in soothing inflammation.

The most commonly used herbal remedies are Essiac, Iscador, aloe vera, P C Spes and Carctol, which are believed to support the body in its fight against cancer. Lymph-drainage herbs, chest herbs, menopause herbs, and liver herbs can also be taken for general systemic support. These are available through the Bristol Cancer Help Centre Shop, Argyll Herbs, or Nature's Own (*see* Appendix II). Iscador is a prescription-only medicine and is available through homoeopathic hospitals, Dr Andrew Maendl in Bristol, or anthroposophical doctors and The Park Attwood Centre in Worcestershire (*see* Appendix II).

## Alternative cancer medicines

Alternative medicines for cancer have come to be defined as therapies that are used instead of, rather than along with, conventional medicine, and the practitioners using them view as a treatment for cancer in their own right. Usually they are aimed at restoring immune function and metabolic integrity, and for detoxification.

A number of alternative cancer clinics specialize in a range of therapies of this type, namely the Gerson and Contreras Clinics (which have now amalgamated as the Oasis Centre), and the

Stella Maris Clinics under Dr Alberto Gilvarez, both in Mexico, the Bad Steben and Bad Aibling Clinics in Bavaria, and the clinics of the alternative cancer doctors that are practising in Britain. (*See* Appendix II.)

Treatments usually involve extensive testing to establish the state of the body's toxicity and immune mechanism; then the body is treated, usually by intravenous drip, with a large range of detoxifying and immune-boosting substances. The treatment will normally be supplemented with a diet of very high-quality food. These metabolic approaches are seen by many as the ideal alternative to chemotherapy before or during the process of embarking upon psycho-spiritual healing. They may also be used to revive the body after chemotherapy and radiotherapy.

There is currently a trend towards the use of hyperthermia treatment for cancer; with this, heat or electrical currents are used to shrink or destroy tumours. The treatment is available from Professor Douwes in Germany, and from Dr Fritz Schellander in England.

## The Self-help Techniques used at Bristol

Once energy levels are restored through holistic therapy, the next step is embarking upon a self-help programme in order to consolidate the benefits achieved through therapy and to go on building the strength of body, mind and spirit.

### Exercise

Once you are strong enough you may wish to replace or augment body work and energy medicines with Eastern exercise practices, which keep the energy flow moving and balanced. These are the systems of t'ai chi, chi gong and yoga – all wonderfully integrated holistic practices that stimulate the body and rebalance the system, keep the *chi* flowing in the body, and clear the mind, engendering an extremely peaceful state of being.

Within yoga there is a sub-speciality called 'pranayama', which is very specialized breathwork. This can be enormously helpful for people with breathing problems, and for anyone who has a great need to calm their nervous system and to re-energize themselves. Swimming and walking are also encouraged in order to develop strength and stamina.

## Mind–body techniques

The other extremely important self-help techniques are the mind–body techniques of relaxation, meditation and visualization. Overall these techniques have the effect of lessening the grip of fear in our bodies and minds, so that the spirit lifts and the body is able to relax and heal. There can be a tendency for these specialities to blur into one, but in reality they are very different and should be treated as such because they all have extremely important therapeutic values.

## Relaxation

Relaxation is the process by which tension is released from the physical body; and it involves sequential release of muscular tension until the body becomes limp and feels heavy. During this process you will tend automatically to move into very unfocused, pleasant states of mind. Relaxation exercises should be performed while lying down in a warm, comfortable, peaceful environment where you will not be disturbed.

## Meditation

In meditation the emphasis is on stilling the mind. The body is usually positioned in an upright balanced posture, and the mind is alert and awake with a single point of focus; which can be either a sound, an image or the sensation of the rise and fall of the breath. This practice has extremely profound consequences. Normally our minds are full of our thoughts, feelings, emotions and sensations, and our consciousness is obscured by these . All the religions of the world have meditation as their central process.

It is stated within the Bible that 'the kingdom of Heaven is within'. By this is meant that the underlying nature of our consciousness is bliss or joy, in which we have a sense of being connected to, or one with, all creation. This type of consciousness is there all the time behind the habitual patterns of panic, anxiety, and the preoccupation with our feelings and thoughts. This is analogous to our consciousness being the blue sky that is always present behind the cloud layers. As we begin to meditate, the cloud layer gradually breaks up and we begin to see glimpses of the blue sky. The more we practise, the more the cloud layer begins to disappear, and every now and again the sun comes out, which is analogous to our connecting to our higher consciousness or the divinity that is within us.

The more we practise meditation the more we automatically go into happier, calmer, more reflective states of mind. In PNI terms we could not possibly be doing anything better for our bodies. We are effectively replacing the neuropeptide cocktail,which is associated with our rather chaotic, fearful states of mind, with a beautiful, clear state in which we know very deeply that all is well and begin to understand our true relationship with life. The message that this gives to our tissues is profoundly healing and indeed there is a healing centre in Australia, called the Yarra Valley Living Centre (*see* Appendix II), whose work is based very centrally around the healing of cancer through meditation. This is because its founder, Ian Gawler, had a spectacular recovery from secondary bone cancer, having learned how to get into extremely deep, prolonged meditative states from his teacher, Dr Ainsley Meares.

## Visualization

Visualization is another technique altogether. It is what is often described colloquially as 'mind over matter', i.e. using the power of the mind to change reality.

The practice of visualization shows us that our perception of reality depends very much on what we think. For most of us, what we are thinking and believing about the way things will be is an unconscious activity. This means that a great deal of what happens to us is determined by our unconscious beliefs or attitudes, yet we blame external factors for the situations that we find ourselves in.

> I didn't have a great many options to recover from my tumour since I turned down orthodox medicine, but of the various alternatives offered to me visualization appealed the most because I've always believed in the power of the mind. So it was visualization that caught on with me. Then it was a question of deciding which of the different sorts of visualization I would use for my particular problem. I've always loved the sun so that had to be involved. I relaxed each day for about two to three years, and pictured myself lying in the sun. The venue was a lovely sandy beach, with palm trees, in some far-off country. I lay on the beach listening to the sea lapping the shore. I felt the rays of the sun and felt them healing and actually shrinking the tumour. This I continued to do. I went back for various check-ups over the years, and on each occasion it was found that the tumour had shrunk. In the end there was no tumour at all – just a bit of scar tissue from the biopsy. And here I am now, and it's 12 years since I was given just a few weeks to live.
>
> *Audrey Parcell: Living with inoperable lymphoma,*
> *first diagnosed in 1987*

In the process of visualization we are making conscious choices about the outcomes we want. In the context of illness this means having images of the body completely healed; images of our self strong and whole again, and images of the way things will be in our life, imagining ourselves being present at specific events in the future. We can make specific choices and goals for ourselves, which will greatly enhance the likelihood of these things coming to pass. These techniques are used in business and sports all the time, with measurable improvements in outcome.

A frequent problem occurs when a doctor, who represents the voice of authority, predicts the likely outcome of an illness on the basis of statistics. This can create a very strong negative visualization, and often people will fulfil the prophecy almost to the day if a prognosis has been given in terms of years or months to live. In this situation new images, which allow for the possibility of survival and recovery, have to be created. Some people use very combative images, seeing their cancer smashed up, destroyed or attacked. Others use gentle transformative images like sun, wind, light or water, melting, dissolving, blowing or washing the illness away, seeing their body completely cleared of cancer after every visualization. (*See* Chapter 5.)

This personal imagery or visualization is different from the process of guided visualization in which a therapist leads you into a gentle, imaginative, pleasant frame of mind, giving comforting, loving and beautiful images to induce a great state of well-being that produces very positive PNI changes. Experienced, psychotherapeutically trained guides can also use this technique to do therapeutic work with individuals or groups, to help access the emotional plane and inner wisdom.

It is possible to use these techniques to initiate dialogue with the wounded or ill part of oneself directly, asking it what is wrong and what it needs, developing in this way an extremely real relationship with the body. However, it must be stressed that this is psychotherapeutic work for which it is necessary to have a properly trained psychotherapist facilitator, so that what is brought up to consciousness can be processed and integrated for your healing.

## Spiritual enquiry

Spiritual enquiry often becomes activated if there is serious life-threatening illness. The kind of questions that come to the surface are:

- What is life all about?
- Is there a purpose to life or is this all there is?
- If there is a purpose, what is it and how does it affect me?
- If it is a journey, where am I going?
- Is there any sense in it all?
- What will happen to me when I die?

Throughout centuries people have asked these questions. All spiritual teachers tell us that often, through the very process of asking and thinking about these questions, and working on the areas of our faith, belief and understanding, the inner spiritual essence within us awakens, and with this awakening a huge amount of energy for living life in the here and now is released.

Application of the holistic approach helps us develop our spiritual awareness and consciousness, giving us a greater understanding of the whole life process. With support and healing, individuals often arrive at the belief or knowing that they come from love and that they circle back round to love, on a great adventure of living with all its ups and downs. They know they are spiritual beings in physical bodies and that ultimately they are safe, even in death. This realization makes the whole context of the life process something quite different. Illness becomes a wake-up call and a time to remember who we really are spiritually; and this remembering and spiritual awakening frees us to live fully and passionately in the moment. This spiritual awakening can cause what Deepak Chopra calls 'quantum healing': an acute sense of excitement, which is itself extremely healing, as great energy and joy are liberated, enabling us to experience a very great sense of aliveness and peace – even if death is quite imminent.

# PART FOUR

# LOOKING FORWARD

## 11

# *The Future for the Holistic Approach to Cancer*

Many people who embark upon the holistic approach to cancer are at some point likely to suffer from a considerable sense of frustration: not with the approach itself but with the amount of leg work they have to do in order to find out about complementary, alternative and self-help therapies. Indeed, many have said that in the six weeks post diagnosis they feel they must have done enough work to warrant a PhD in the subject.

Clearly a lot more work needs to be done to integrate the different approaches to cancer so that a great deal of this burden can be taken away from people with cancer, who are after all in shock and distress and can do without having to expend such energy and effort in researching their options. It is also vital to make sure that the relevant information gets to people who do not have the facilities or experience to begin such a big research project.

## The Integrated Cancer Services of the Future

Many cancer centres and units are taking active steps towards building support services into the system. These services revolve mainly around providing counselling, support groups and complementary therapies to help people deal with their shock, distress and symptoms. What has not yet happened, however, is the adoption of the health promotion aspect of the Bristol Approach in any hospital setting. In other words, whilst there is wide-scale acceptance of the idea that complementary therapies help people to feel better, there is still concern that getting people with cancer involved in efforts to improve their health is questionable. The possible benefits of this involvement are seen, in some medical quarters, as being outweighed by the risk of creating in patients feelings of over-responsibility for the illness and recovery process, which in turn may bring about self-blame.

There is no cancer unit I know of yet that has the made this paradigm shift to encourage the involvement of people with cancer in the promotion of their own health through holistic approaches. I am quite convinced that taking this step would lead to far better outcomes from medical treatments and – as people became more self-reliant – decreased demand on cancer healthcare professionals. It is even likely that there would be a decrease in the cost of cancer medicine as people actively choose holistic self-help options rather than very expensive surgical, chemo and radio regimes for late-stage cancer.

## The ideal integrated service

My ideal integrated cancer service would provide immediate support to help people cope with the intense emotional reaction that invariably follows cancer diagnosis. They would be given time to recover from the shock, and then a process of examining all the options – both conventional and holistic – would be undertaken.

If conventional medicine was the treatment of choice then complementary medical care would be given to prepare people for, support them through, and help them after, their treatment protocol. If an alternative route was chosen, medical monitoring, to check on progress, could be given regularly in the same way that it is before and after conventional treatments. This would be done without judgement, and without blame or ridicule if these treatments were not successful. Let's face it, conventional medical treatments for cancer are not always successful either. Once the process of 'disease management' had been undertaken the bigger process of holistic health promotion would begin in the way it has been described in this book.

**Information and access**
Within the hospital where the diagnosis was made there would be first-class information services. These would inform people on all aspects of cancer and cancer care, including:

- The cancer itself.
- The treatment of cancer.
- Medical frontier treatments and developments.
- Conventional cancer care services.
- Holistic cancer services.
- Support services.
- Legal, social and financial services.
- Cancer prevention.

They would also help you to contact 'cancer buddies' – people who have the same sort of cancer as you, and with whom you could benefit from mutual support and understanding.

The people running the information service would be unbiased, and would be set up in such a way that it would be clear whether the evidence for the efficacy of a given treatment is:

- scientific (based on the results of controlled tests or studies); or
- anecdotal (based on the testimony or experience of other patients); or
- theoretical (based on the possibly sound hypotheses of a practitioner or scientist, but as yet unproven).

Within these units it would be possible to arrange appointments with doctors or nurses that have studied the full range of different approaches to cancer; they would therefore be able to help individuals assess their clinical, emotional and mental state, and their health values and beliefs, so enabling them to choose the treatments and/or therapies that are best suited to them.

Having made the choices and embarked on a course of action, the individual would have continuous access to link workers, who would provide practical support and help throughout the cancer journey, passing the relevant information between consultants, general practitioners, nurse support agencies, and those involved in the holistic care of the individual. These link workers would also, from the beginning, make an assessment of the individual's social situation, taking special care to ensure that a support network was set in place for those who are particularly isolated or psychologically vulnerable.

An emergency 24-hour helpline, and drop-in centres, designed around the support and self-help needs of people with cancer, and running seven days a week, would be available to provide emotional support and practical advice on demand.

Ideally the drop-in centre would be based away from the hospital, in the heart of the local community, forming a bridge between the places where people live and work and the hospital environment. At the same time, residential holistic programmes would be offered countrywide in specialist centres like the Bristol Cancer Help Centre.

## Making it happen

To make this degree of flexibility possible, it would be essential for all those involved in the care of people with cancer to learn about the full range of alternatives available so that they could come to respect and promote the values upon which holistic and psychological options are based. Most important of all, it would be necessary for healthcare professionals to open themselves up to allowing the person's value system to be the dominant one, and to undertake routine training in communication skills and basic psychology so that the most fundamental need of those in their care – the need for an empathic, trusting relationship with carers – can be met by all healthcare professionals.

If you like the sound of this model, communicate it in your own words to your local services director and manager. They are supposed to listen to their users, and unless you tell them how you would like the service to be it will stay as it is now.

## Differences and Developments in the Holistic Approach

Another frustration for people with cancer is brought about by the current divide between the predominantly psycho-spiritual services of the Bristol Cancer Help Centre and the metabolic alternative cancer clinics in Germany and Mexico and scattered around Britain. This means that people embarking upon the holistic approach may have to travel a great deal and spend a lot of money in order to include both aspects of holistic medicine.

This problem was brought to light in several cancer conferences during 1999. As a result it is likely that there will be an acceleration in the development of metabolic treatment clinics in Great Britain where people can go as an in-patient for residential stays. Currently the fort is being held in the UK by Dr Patrick Kingsley in Leicester, Dr Fritz Shellander in Tunbridge Wells, and Doctors Rajendra Sharma, Etienne Callibout, Hugh Cox and Adeni Jones, all in London. All these practitioners are working on an out-patient basis. Work is going on under the direction of Carol Eastman, at Lynden Hill Clinic in Reading, to establish in-patient alternative cancer treatment facilities in the UK.

## Potential Cross-over Areas between Orthodox and Complementary Medicine

In the future, it is very likely that science will increasingly substantiate the value of the holistic approach in coping with cancer, and this will mean that it will become increasingly incorporated into mainstream care. It is likely, for example, that research will show us exactly which of the phytochemicals contained in particular vegetables and other plants have cancer-preventative and cancer-treatment properties. If this happens it will not be long before these substances are extracted or synthesized chemically by the pharmaceutical industry for use in drugs for cancer treatment or prevention (*see* box below).

Another cross-over area is likely to occur as a result of future advances in the area of psychoneuroimmunology (PNI). In the fullness of time it will no doubt become clear exactly which sorts of mental state in which kind of people weaken immune function and, conversely, exactly which states and techniques can optimize immune function. No doubt it will also be possible very soon to measure very accurately an individual's immune status so that the need for – and effectiveness of – psychosomatic therapeutic interventions can be gauged. This will also be a major step forward in terms of cancer prevention because people will then be able to make a very accurate assessment of the degree to which they are at risk from cancer and other diseases.

---

### The anti-cancer snack?

As a sign of things to come, perhaps, the Tenovus Institute in Cardiff has made a snack-bar called 'Prevacan', with the advice that a bar of Prevacan eaten daily will strongly reduce the risk of breast cancer. Amongst this bar's ingredients are seeds and grains that include high levels of diadzein and genistein, which are phytochemicals believed to protect against breast cancer. These phytochemicals are found in high levels in the diet of Japanese women, who have a four times lower life-time risk of suffering from breast cancer than do Western women. Of course, all the substances contained in the snack-bar are obtained anyway by eating a wholefood diet.

---

To date, the difficulty in assessing the effect of psychological state on health is that individuals can apparently be experiencing the same levels of stress, distress, or trauma, and yet respond differently: some will cope while others crumble. Suzanne Kabosa, who has studied this area, has called the ability to withstand stress 'personality hardiness', typified by people who respond to stress as an energizing challenge rather than as a crushing problem.

## Research

Whilst the developments we have looked at so far are quite likely to come to fruition, it is vital that high-quality medical research is done on the many alternative medical treatments for cancer, the holistic approach as used at Bristol, and integrated approaches for supportive care and symptom management, which are increasingly being used in hospitals and hospices. Good progress is being made in this area by the American Office of Alternative Medicine, Cancer Research Department.

The thing that will expedite this most is the development of some meaningful outcome measures by which the many benefits experienced by those that use the holistic approach can be assessed. We could then use the information to make more accurate judgements, and perhaps even predictions, which would enable people to make even more informed choices about their treatment and care.

It is also important that those involved in mainstream cancer care take more notice of the results of qualitative studies in which people with cancer express their views about their needs, the types of service they want, and what they consider to be the most pressing priorities for research. For example, women with breast cancer who took part in a study conducted in Australia said that their research priorities lay in the area of cancer prevention, followed by psycho-social care and holistic help for people with cancer. Whilst they wanted medical research into the disease itself, they felt more strongly that what was happening to them must be prevented for future generations.

As it is, it is research into medical cancer treatment, and into the nature of cancer itself, that is almost invariably at the top of the mainstream research agenda of healthcare professionals and research agencies. Around 90 per cent of research is done on the disease itself, while only 10 per cent is being put into prevention and care. People who actually have cancer would generally like to see a 40/60 balance, with the main emphasis on prevention.

## The Prevention of Cancer

It is extremely humbling to know that in so many cases the main concern of people with cancer is the prevention of the disease rather than its cure. Certainly, in working at Bristol, it is now clear to me that what has been learned over the years in pioneering the holistic approach to cancer must now be applied urgently to the prevention of cancer in society. As 70 per cent of deaths from cancer are thought to be caused by poor diet, smoking and alcohol, and a further 10 per cent are the result of infection, cancer can most definitely be seen as a primarily preventable disease.[16]

It is high time that all possible effort was put into tackling the prevention of this appalling disease, which is affecting one in four of us and killing one in three. Whilst there are serious environmental factors that affect the degree of risk – and these issues need to be addressed, too – it is essential that we focus on what we as an individuals can do to reduce the risk of cancer in ourselves and those that are close to us.

The almost-universal cry from those that have attended the year-long programme at Bristol has been, 'Why, oh why did I have to get cancer before I could discover this absolutely wonderful process of getting my life and health back on track?' Many have said that everyone should have the opportunity of learning about, and embarking on, the holistic approach to health. And, of course, there is no reason why everyone shouldn't. The approach described in this book is as relevant for those wishing to prevent cancer – or simply to enjoy a higher quality of life and health – as it is for those wishing to heal it.

So whether you are reading this book as someone with cancer, as a supporter of someone with cancer, or simply as someone who would like to take steps towards preventing cancer, the crucial step is to commit yourself to embarking upon the holistic approach to health. As with most things in life, the most important – and sometimes the most difficult – step is the first. But, in committing yourself to your life and your health, you will find that the benefits are directly proportionate to your input.

This is perhaps best summed up in Goethe's famous words on the subject of commitment:

> Until there is commitment, there is hesitancy.
> The chance to draw back, always ineffectiveness.
> Concerning all acts of initiative (and creation)
> There is one elementary truth, the ignorance of which
> Kills countless ideas and splendid plans:
> That the moment that one definitely commits oneself,
> Then providence moves too.
> All sorts of things occur to help one that would never
> Otherwise have occurred.
> A whole stream of events issues forth from the decision
> Raising in one's favour all manner of unforeseen
> Incidents and meetings and material assistance,
> Which no man could have dreamed would have come his way.
> Whatever you can do or dream you can, begin it.
> Boldness has genius, power and magic in it.
> Begin it now.

And may we at the Bristol Cancer Help Centre encourage you wholeheartedly to take the crucial steps described in this book to improve your own health and well-being, and wish you all power, courage, blessings, and our love, as you embark on your own unique healing journey.

# *Appendix I: Recipes*

Many foods have been shown to have a pharmacological effect on the body. Mushrooms and garlic both support the immune system, balance hormone activity, improve liver function, and inhibit damage to DNA and the excessive cell growth that can precede cancer. Shitake mushrooms in particular boost interferon levels and increase interleukin activity, and are rich in a range of polysaccharides. Ginger is rich in antioxidants and improves production of glutathione-s-transferase, a key enzyme responsible for detoxification. Organic miso is high in beneficial bacteria, and soya products are known for their health support. For this reason, the recipes here include many, if not all, of these important foods.

## Supportive Soup

10 fresh (or dried) shitake mushrooms
3–4 in (7–10 cm) fresh ginger-root, grated
4 big cloves of garlic, grated
6 tsp miso paste
6 spring onions, finely sliced
3 pints water

Simmer everything together – except the miso and onions – for 30 minutes. Add miso, and allow it to melt gently for 5 minutes. Then add onions, and serve.

# Spiced Bean Paté

225 g (10 oz/1½ cups) beans (aduki, pinto, barlotti, cannelli)
6 cloves garlic, peeled
1 large onion, finely chopped
1 red or green pepper, finely chopped
2 tbsp olive oil
1 tsp ground cumin
1 tsp paprika or pimiento
1 tsp ground black pepper
2 tsp tamari

1. Place the beans and four of the garlic cloves in a pan with some water, and cook until very soft. Then mash with a potato-masher, fork, or in a food-processor, and set aside.
2. Sauté the remaining two garlic cloves, the onion and the chopped pepper, in the oil over a gentle heat until soft. Stir in the spices. Fry for another few minutes, and then add the tamari and the black pepper.
3. Add the bean mixture, and mash together. Press into six ramekin pots or a bowl, and leave to cool.

Delicious served with hot bread or toast as a first course, or as a sandwich filling.

# Provençal Vegetables

Serves 4–6

3 tbsp olive oil
1 large onion
2 large garlic cloves
1 tsp dried oregano
1 tsp dried thyme
3 tbsp tomato purée/paste
4 ripe tomatoes
1 aubergine (eggplant), chopped
3 medium courgettes (zucchini), chopped
1 green or red pepper, chopped
1 tsp ground black pepper
1 tbsp tamari

1. Heat the oil in a large, heavy-based pan with a lid. Add the onion, garlic cloves, oregano and thyme, and heat until softened.
2. Add the tomato purée, and stir over a medium heat for a few minutes until the oil begins to separate itself from the mixture. Add the remaining ingredients.
3. When the mixture is sizzling, reduce the heat, cover, and simmer very gently for 35–40 minutes, either on the stove or in the oven (180°C/350°F/gas mark 4).
4. Uncover, and cook for a further 5 minutes to reduce a little of the liquid, stirring as necessary.

# Poppy Seed and Sour 'Cream' Pasta

225 g (8 oz/2½ cups) wholewheat pasta
85 ml (3fl oz/⅓ cup) lemon juice
2 tbsp olive oil
1 tbsp miso paste
1 tbsp tamari soy sauce
225 g (8 oz/1 cup) tofu
15 g (½oz/⅓ cup) chopped fresh chives
25g (1 oz/¼ cup) poppy seeds
½ tsp paprika
Ground black pepper to taste

1. Cook pasta until tender, drain, and set aside.
2. Place the lemon juice, olive oil, miso paste, tamari soy sauce, tofu and fresh chives in a food-processor, and blend until smooth. (If you use a blender, you may need to add a little water to keep it moving.)
3. Stir the seeds and creamy mix into the pasta. Turn into a greased, ovenproof dish, sprinkle with some pepper and paprika, and bake in a moderate oven for about 20 minutes.

Delicious with baked courgettes or a tomato and onion salad. Poppy seeds have a high calcium content.

# Middle Eastern Rice Salad

350 g (12 oz/2 cups) cooked brown rice
6 chopped dates, dried or fresh
4  tbsp toasted cashew nuts
4 spring onions, finely sliced
2 tbsp Tamari soy sauce
1 tbsp toasted fennel seeds
1 tbsp toasted cumin seeds
juice of 1 juicy lemon
3 tbsp olive oil

Gently mix all the ingredients together. Set to one side to 'develop' for about 30 minutes, and then serve.

The nutrients contained in this salad are very well balanced. The recipe can be adapted using any cooked whole grain, and served hot or cold with dressings and imaginative mixtures of fruit, veggies, nuts and seeds.

# Fresh Tomato and Basil Dressing

2 large fresh, ripe tomatoes
1 tbsp cider vinegar
2 tbsp olive oil (optional)
Generous handful fresh basil leaves and stalks
½ tsp black pepper
2 tsp tamari

Just whizz the ingredients together in a blender until smooth.

This is great on cooked or raw vegetables. For extra zing, add a chopped red pepper – roasted or not. Try experimenting with more oil-free dressings in this style.

## Date and Banana Cookies

75 g (3oz/½ cup) dried dates, finely chopped
75 g (3oz/⅔ cup) walnuts, finely chopped
3 medium bananas, mashed
175 g (6oz/2 cups) oats
100 ml (⅖ cup) olive oil
1 tsp vanilla essence

Mix together really well and put tablespoons of the mixture onto an oiled baking sheet. Flatten them down a bit, and bake in a moderate oven for about 20 minutes, until golden.

## Jelly without Gelatine

1 (heaped) tbsp agar agar flakes
   (If you are using powdered agar agar, use sufficient for 1 pint, as specified on the packet)
⅔ pint water
⅓ pint natural fruit syrup or extract

1. Heat the flakes and half the water together in a small saucepan, and allow to boil for 4 or 5 minutes, whisking well as the mixture boils and froths.
2. Whisk into the natural fruit syrup and the remaining water.
3. Pour mixture into a bowl or glasses, and allow to set.

Unlike gelatine, agar will set quickly at room temperature. You can make delicious desserts using freshly juiced fruits.

# *Appendix II:*
# *Useful Contacts*

**Bristol Cancer Help Centre**
Reception: 0117 980 9500
Helpline: 0117 980 9505
Shop: 0117 980 9504
Bookings: 0117 980 9050

**Dr Rosy Daniel**
Consultation: London 020 7299 9428
               Bristol 0117 980 9521

## Therapies

*Acupuncture*
British Council of Acupuncture: 020 8735 0400.

*Art therapy*
British Association of Art Therapists: 01710 383 3774.

*Counselling*
British Association of Counsellors: 01788 578328.
Centre for Transpersonal Psychology: 020 7935 7350.

## Healing
National Federation of Spiritual Healers: Referral Service, 0891 616080.
White Eagle Lodge: 01730 893300.

## Homoeopathy
Society of Homoeopaths: 01604 621400.

## Massage
Massage Therapy Institute Register: Andy Fagg, 0117 661008.

## Music therapy
MusicSpace: 0117 976 2734; 0117 973 2105.

## Reflexology
British Reflexology Association: 01886 821207.

## Shiatsu
Shiatsu Society: 01733 758341.

# Self-Help Approaches

## Buddhism
Friends of the Western Buddhist Order: 0117 924 9991.

## Chi gong
Zhi Xing Wang: 020 7229 7187.

## Meditation
Transcendental Meditation Centre: 0990 143 733.

## Relaxation
Relaxation for Living: 01983 868166.

## *T'ai chi*
Rising Dragon T'ai Chi: Richard Farmer, 01432 840282.

## *Tantra*
Sky Dancing Tantra (UK): 01736 759050.

## *Yoga*
British Wheel of Yoga: 01529 306851.

# Alternative Approaches

## *Allergies*
Brakespeare Hospital: Dr Jean Munroe, 01442 261333.

## *Diet*
Gerson Diet: Lesley Pearce, 01372 817652.

## *Stress*
Geopathic Stress: for advice and information about practitioners in your area, Ann and Roy Proctor, 01458 223 215.

# Treatment and Support Services

## *Cancer information and support services*
Cancer Alternative Information Bureau: 020 7266 1505.
CancerBACUP: Cancer and its Treatment, 0808 800 1234.
Cancer Link: Support Groups, 0800 132905.
Haven Trust: Support: 020 7384 0000.
Marie-Curie Nurses: for nursing help ask your GP; head office; 020 7235 3325.
Macmillan Cancer Relief: for nursing help ask your GP; information line, 0845 601 6161.

## Residential alternative cancer treatment centres in Britain

Royal Homoeopathic Hospital: London, 020 7837 8833.
Lyndon Hill Clinic: 0118 940 1234.
Park Attwood Anthroposophical Clinic: 01299 861 444.

## Alternative cancer treatment websites

Type 'alternative cancer' or 'holistic cancer' into your Internet
browser.

## Doctors and clinics offering alternative cancer treatments

### Britain:

Dr Ali: The Integrated Medical Centre (Ayurveda), London,
020 7224 5111.
Dr Hugh Cox: Aylesbury, 01296 399 317.
Dr Etienne Callebout: London, 020 7935 6593.
Dr Jan de Vries: 01292 311414.
Dr Julian Kenyon: 01703 334752.
Dr Patrick Kingsley: Leicestershire, 01530 223622.
Dr George Lewith: Southampton, 01703 334752.
Dr Roger Lichy: Bristol and London, 08700 780 560.
Dr Fritz Schellander: Liongate Clinic, 01892 543 535.
Dr Rajendra Sharma: London and Guildford, 01425 461740.

### Outside Britain

Professor Douwes: Germany, 49 8061 494217.
Dr Michael Schachter: New York, USA, 914 368 4700.
Dr Gilberto Alvarez: Mexico, 5266 3434 44.
HYPERLINK mail to: Stellamaris@altavista.net
HYPERLINK http://www.stellamanisclinic.com
Dr Alexander Herzog: Klinic Bendiktus Guelle, Germany, 9604
6840.

A comprehensive list of cancer treatment centres can be found
in *The Definitive Guide to Cancer,* by John Diamond, W. Lee and
Burton Goldberg (*see* Further Reading).

## International holistic centres

Ian Gawler: The Yarra Valley Living Centre, Melbourne, Australia, 613 596 71730.

Darinka Gomiscek: Slovenia, 0038 665 25338.

Tara McInty: The Sanctuary, Victoria, Australia, 052 584 562/052 226 969/052 226 966.

Dr Michael Lerner: Commomwheel, California, USA, 415 868 0970.

Dr Nimrod Sheinman: Tel Aviv, Israel, 972 9 8991497.

Dr Michael Wetzler: Capetown, South Africa, 0027 21 762 6215.

## Retreats

The Sacred Space Foundation: 01768 898 375.

# Research

## Cancer research and frontier medical information

Cancer Research Campaign (CRC): 0800 226 237.

Imperial Cancer Research Fund (ICRF): 020 7269 3611.

Institute of Cancer Research (ICR): 0800 731 9468.

American Cancer Society: New York, USA, 212 586 8700.

Sloane Kettering Memorial Cancer Centre, USA, 001 212 639 7972.

## Complementary medical research

Research Council for Complementary Medicine (RCCM): 02073 841772.
HYPERLINK http://www.rccm.org.uk
www.rccm.org.uk

The American Centre for Alternative Medicine Research: HYPERLINK http://www.sph.uth.tmc.edu/utcam

# Suppliers

The Bristol Cancer Help Centre Shop: 0117 980 9504 (1–6pm).
Various books, tapes and videos, plus vitamin and mineral supplements, are available by mail order from the shop. All profits from the Centre Shop go to the Centre's charity.

Nature's Own: 01684 310099.
Suppliers of raffa water, aloe vera, etc., by mail-order.

Chard Natural Health: 01460 62953.

Aerobic oxygen: Philip Barker, 01725 513129.

PC Spes Botanics: 001 516 432 1758.

Argyll Herbs: Ute Brookman, 01934 863353.

Higher Nature: 01435 883484.

The Nutri Centre, Hale Clinic, London 020 7631 0156.

Galen Homoeopathics: 01305 263 996.
Homoeopathic medicine and radiation remedy.

# Holistic Support Groups in Britain

### Bristol
SASH Support and Self-Help,
8 Giffords Place, Bristol BS13 7GP.
*Contact*: Sandy Evans, 0117 935 8880.

### Cambridgeshire
Cambridge Cancer Help Centre,
1a Stockwell Street, Off Mill Road Cambridge CB1 3DD.
*Contact*: Anne Dingley, 01223 566151.

### Cheshire
Macclesfield & District Cancer Support Group,
29 Meadow Drive, Prestbury Macclesfield SK10 4EY.
*Contact*: Jennifer Round, 01625 828961.

## Cornwall
Camborne/Redruth Cancer Support Group,
Well-being Centre, Old School House, Illogan, Redruth TR16 4SW.
*Contact*: Gerald Wartna, 01726 843576.

## Cumbria
Gentle Approach to Cancer Association,
Nebblethwaite Hall, Sedbergh LA10 5LX.
*Contact*: Liz Newsom 01539 621307.

## Devon
Tavistock Cancer Support Group,
c/o Social Services Tavistock District Abbey Rise, Whitchurch Road, Tavistock PL19 9AS.
*Contact*: Rhoda Cansick 01822 613082 (early morning, lunchtime, evenings).

## Dorset
Bridport Healing and Cancer Care Centre,
The Friends Meeting House, 95 South Street Bridport DT6 3ND.
*Contact*: Joan Waterfall 01308 422459 (after 6.00 p.m.).

## Essex
North East London Cancer Help,
Sue's House, 10 Dawlish Drive, Ilford IG3 9ED.
*Contact*: Frank Longcroft, 020 8597 0024 (10.30 a.m.–4.00 p.m.)

## Galway
Slanu Galway Cancer Help Centre,
Unit 6, Ballybane Industrial Estate, Ballybane Republic of Ireland.
*Contact*: Eileen Joyce-Henelly, 00 353 91 755023.

**Hampshire**
Emsworth Cancer Support Group,
31 Horndean Road, Emsworth PO10 7PU.
*Contact*: Joan Wiggins, 01243 377913.

**Hertfordshire**
Stevenage Cancer Support Group,
23 Boswell Gardens, Stevenage SG1 4SB.
*Contact*: Lynda McGilvray, 01438 352793.

**Isle of Man**
Manx Cancer Help Association,
Laurel Cottage, Main Road, Crosby IM4 4BL.
*Contact*: Eve Berridge, 01624 852825.

**Kent**
ABACUS The Cancer Self-Help Support Group,
16 Southwood Close, Bromley, BR1 2LU.
*Contact*: Ray Bailey, 020 8467 2565 (8.00 a.m.–10.30 p.m).

Bearstead Holistic Cancer and Stress Self-Help and Support
  Centre,
Lavender Cottage, Bearstead Road, Maidstone ME14 5LD.
*Contact*: Kathleen Wingrove, 01622 730133 (after 4.00 p.m.).

**Lancashire**
CancerVIVE Gentle Approach to Cancer Association,
272 Norbreck Road, Thornton Cleveleys FY5 1PA.
*Contact*: Phil Moran 01253 864655.

Lancashire Gentle Approach to Cancer Association,
11 Lambert Road, Ribbleton, Preston PR2 6YQ.
*Contact*: Colin Sutherland, 01772 705465.

## London
The Cancer Resource Centre,
P.O. Box 17, 20–22 York Road, Wandsworth SW11 3QE.
*Contact*: Petra Griffiths, 020 7924 3924 (Monday, Wednesday and Thursday).

## North Yorkshire
Yorkshire Cancer Help Centre,
3 Station View, Harrogate, NG2 7JA.
*Contact*: Ann Scott, 0113 216 8894.

## Northumberland
Cancer Support Group,
16 Leazes Crescent, Hexham NE46 3JZ.
*Contacts*: Pat Fogg, 0191 410 2679; Betty Heslop, 01434 684337; Linda Brinkhurst, 01661 842919.

## Nottinghamshire
Mansfield Self-Help Cancer Group,
196 Chesterfield Road South, Mansfield, NG17 7EE.
*Contact*: Sheila Orange, 01623 624632.

## Powys
The Melangell Centre,
Pennant Melangell, Llangynog, Nr Oswestry SY10 0HQ.
*Contact*: Judith Prust 01691 860408.

## Surrey
New Approaches to Cancer,
St Peters Hospital, Guildford Road, Chertsey KT16 0PZ.
*Contact*: Colin Ryder Richardson, 0800 389 2662.

South East Cancer Help Centre,
2 Purley Road Tesco Development, Purley Cross CR8 2HA.
*Contact*: Kathy Behan 020 8668 0974 (helpline).

**Swansea**
Swansea Cancer Self-Help Group,
10 Vivians Row, Pantlasau, Morriston SA6 6NS.
*Contact*: Valerie Johnson, 01792 794233.

**West Sussex**
Crawley Cancer Contact,
1 Heron Way, Horsham RH13 6DF.
*Contact*: Heather Goodare, 01403 261674.

Wessex Cancer Help Centre,
8 South Street, Chichester PO19 1EH.
*Contact*: Betty Deal 01243 778516 (Monday to Friday 9.30
a.m.–1.00 p.m.).

**West Yorkshire**
Natural Healing Group,
Yorkshire Regional Oncology Unit, Hospital Lane, Leeds.
*Contact*: Ruth Kaye, 0113 268 5724.

# Notes

1.  Greer, S., et al., 'Psychological response to breast cancer and 15 year outcome', from *Lancet* (1990), Vol. 335, p. 49.
2.  Spiegel, D., 'Effect of psycho-social treatment on survival of patients with metastatic breast cancer', from *Lancet* (1989), Vol. 2, p. 888.
3.  Fawzy-Fawzy, et al., 'Malignant melanoma: effects of an early structured psychiatric intervention, coping and affective state on recurrence and survival six years later,' from *Archives of General Psychiatry* (1993), Vol. 50(a), p. 681.
4.  (i) Pert, Candace, *Molecules of Emotion*, Simon & Schuster (1997);
    (ii) Gruzelier, J., Clow, A., Evans, P., Lazar, I., and Walker, L., 'Mind–body influences on immunity: lateralized control, stress, individual difference predictors, and prophylaxis', from *Annals New York Academy of Sciences*.
5.  (i) Daniel, R. and Goodman, S., *Cancer and Nutrition: The Positive Scientific Evidence*, Bristol Cancer Help Centre (1996).
    (ii) The Nutrition Database, Bristol Cancer Help Centre (1996).
6.  Li, J.Y., et al., 'Nutrition trials in Linxian (multiple vitamin/mineral supplementation, cancer incidence, and disease-specific mortality among adults with oesophageal dysplasia)

from *Journal of the National Cancer Institute,* 85.18 (Sept 1993), pp. 1492–98.

7.  (i) Corner, J., Cawley. N., Hildebrand, S., 'An Evaluation of the Use of Massage and Essential Oils on the Well-being of Cancer Patients', from *International Journal of Palliative Nursing* (1995), Vol. 1, No. 2, pp. 67–73;

(ii) Corner, J., Plant, H., A'Hern, R., and Bradley, C. 'Non-Pharmacological Interventions for Breathlessness in Lung Cancer', from *Palliative Medicine* (1996), Vol. 10, pp. 299–305;

(iii) Bredin, M., Corner, J., Krishnasamy, M., Plant, H., Bailey, C., and A'Hern, R., 'Multi-centre randomized controlled trial of nursing intervention for breathlessness in patients with lung cancer', from *British Medical Journal* (April 1999), Vol. 318, pp. 901–4.

8.  Walker, L.G., 'Hypnosis and cancer: Host defences, quality of life, and survival', from *Contemporary Hypnosis* (1998), Vol. 15, No. 1, pp. 34–8.

(i) Ader, R., Fellen, D. and Cohen, N. (eds), *Phoneuroimmunology* (2nd edn), San Diego (1990), Academic Press;

(ii) Kilcott-Glaser, J.K. and Glaser, R., 'Psychoneuroimmunology: can psychological interventions modulate immunity?' from *Journal of Consulting & Clinical Psychology,* 60 (1992), pp569–75.

10.  (i) Drever, F. and Whitehead, M. (eds), *Health Inequalities,* Office for National Statistics, London (1997), The Stationery Office series DS. No. 5;

(ii) Kawacki, et al., 'Social Capital, income inequality and mortality', from *American Journal of Public Health* (1997);

(iii) Davey-Smith, G., et al., 'Explanations for socioeconomic differentials in mortality – evidence from Britain and elsewhere', from *European Journal of Public Health* (1994), 4, pp. 131–44;

(iv) Davey-Smith, G, Shipley, M.J., and Rose, G., 'The magnitude and causes of socio-economic differentials in mortality, further evidence from the Whitehall Study', from *Journal of Epidemiology & Community Health* (1990), 44, pp. 260–5;

(v) *'Our Healthier Nation – a contract for health'* (1998), NHS/Government Report.

11. Goleman, D. and Gurin, J. (eds), *Mind/Body Medicine – How to Use your Mind for Better Health*, Consumer Reports Books.

12. (i) Greer, S., et al, 'Psychological response to breast cancer: effect on outcome', from *Lancet* (1979) ii, pp. 785–7;

(ii) Pettingale, K.W., et al., 'Mental attitudes to cancer: an additional prognostic factor', from *Lancet* 1985, i, p. 750;

(iii) Morris, T., et al., 'Psychological response to cancer diagnosis and disease outcome in patients with breast cancer and lymphoma', from *Psycho-Oncology* (1992), 1, pp. 105–14;

(iv) Hislop, G.T., et al., 'The prognostic significance of psychosocial factors in women with breast cancer', from *Journal of chronic Disease* (1987), 40, pp. 729–35;

(v) Levy, S.M. and Wise, B.D. ,'Psychosocial risk factors and cancer progression', from *Stress & Breast Cancer* (1988), C.L. Cooper (ed.), John Wiley & Sons, Chichester, pp. 77–96.

13. Greer, S., 'Adjuvant psychological therapy for patients with cancer: a prospective randomized controlled trial', from *British Medical Journal* (1992), 304, pp. 675–80.

14. Ornish, D., et al., 'Can lifestyle changes reverse coronary heart disease? The Lifestyle Heart Trial', from *Lancet* (1990), July 21, 336:8708, pp. 129–33.

15. Research Council for Complementary Medicine Database: HYPERLINKhttp://www.rccm.org.uk Tel. 02073 841772

16. Doll & Peto, *Assessment of Environmental Risks* (1975 and 1992), USA,.

17. Thorogood, M., et al., 'Risk of death from cancer and ischaemic heart disease in meat and non-meat eaters', from *British Medical Journal* (1994), Vol. 308, p. 6945.

18. (i) Holm, et al., 'Treatment failure and dietary habits in women with breast cancer', from *Journal of the National Cancer Institute* (1993), Vol. 85, No. 1.6.1.93;
(ii) Lechner and Kronberger, 'Experiences with the use of dietary therapy in surgical oncology', J. Akt. Ernahrmed 15 (1990), 72–8;
(iii) Cohen, L.A., Rose, D.P. and Winder, E.L., 'A rationale for dietary intervention in post-menopausal breast cancer patients – an update in nutrtion and cancer' (1993), pp. 191–10.
19. Dossey, L., *Healing Words* (1996), and *The Power of Prayer*.
20. Benor, D. *Holistic Energy Medicine & Spirituality: Healing Research*, Helix Publishers (ISBN 1 898 271 21 6).
21. Dixon, M., 'Does healing benefit patients with chronic symptoms? A quasi-randomized trial in general practice', from *Journal of the Royal Society of Medicine* (April 1998), Vol. 91.
22. Calman, K. and Hine, D., 'A policy framework for commissioning cancer services; a report of the expert advisory group on cancer to the Chief Medical Officers of England and Wales' (1995), London: Department of Health and Welsh Office.
23. (i) Myers, C.E., et al., 'Adriamycin: the role of lipid peroxidation in cardiac toxicity and tumour response', from *Science* (1977), 197, pp. 165–7;
(ii) Van Vleet, J.F., 'Effects of selenium – Vitamin E on adriamycin induced cardio-myopathy in rabbits' from *J. Vet. Res* (1978), 39, pp. 997–1010;
(iii) Baldew, et al., 'The mechanism of interaction between cisplatin and selenite', from *Bio.Pharm* (1991), Vol. 41, No. 10, pp. 1429–37;
(iv) Lasnitzki, I., 'The influence of A hypervitamins on the effect of 20-methylcholanthrene in mouse prostate glands grown in vitro', from *Br. J.Cancer* (1955), 9, pp. 434–41;
(v) Chopra, D.P. and Wilkoff, L.J., 'Inhibition and reversal

of carcinogen-lesions in mouse prostate in vitro by al-trans-retinoic acid', from *Proc.Am.Assoc.Cancer.Res* (1975), 16, p. 35.

24. Shone, Neville, *Coping Successfully with Pain* (*see* Further Reading).

25. (i) Bridge, L.R, Benson, P., Pietrone, P.C., Purnest, R.G., 'Relaxation and imagery in the treatment of breast cancer', from *British Medical Journal* (1988), 297 (6657), pp. 1169–72;

    (ii) Bindemann, S., Sankop, M., Kaye, S.B., 'Randomized controlled study of relaxation training', from *European Journal of Cancer* (1991), 27 (2), pp. 170–4.

26. Sodegren, K.A., 'The effect of absorption and social closeness on responses to educational and relaxation therapies in patients with anticipatory nausea and vomiting during cancer chemotherapy', from *Dissertation Abstracts International* (1994), 54 (12), p. 6137, University of Minnesota.

27. Louise Brackenbury Radiation Cream (contains no metals), available from Bristol Cancer Help Centre Shop.

28. Rad Brom (which is a generally available homoeopathic remedy) or Galen's Radiation Remedy (available from Bristol Cancer Help Centre Shop).

# Further Reading

All books, video and audio tapes listed here are available from the Bristol Cancer Help Centre Shop, on 0117 980 9504, or on line at www.bristolcancerhelp.org
ISBN numbers are given at the end of each entry.

## Books

*Nutrition*

Daniel, Dr Rosy, *Healing Foods*, Thorsons (1996), 0 7225 3280 6.

Goodman, Dr Sandra, *Nutrition and Cancer: State of the Art*, Positive Health (1998), 0 946170 14 2.

Sen, Jane, *Healing Foods Cookbook*, Thorsons (1996), 0 7225 3322 5.

*The Mind–Body Approach*

Chopra, Deepak, *Quantum Healing*, Bantam (1989), 0 553 173332 4.

LeShan, Lawrence, *Cancer as a Turning Point*, Gateway (1978), 1 85860 046 4.

Martin, Paul, *The Sickening Mind*, Flamingo (1997), 0 00 655022 3.

Myss, Caroline, *Anatomy of the Spirit*, Bantam (1996), 0 553 50527 0.

Pert, Candace, *Molecules of Emotion*, Pocket Books (1997), 0 671 03397 2.

Gawler, Ian, *You Can Conquer Cancer*, Hill of Content (1984), 0 85572 141 3.

## Meditation

Gawler, Ian, *Peace of Mind*, Prism Press (1989), 1 85327 027 X.

LeShan, Lawrence, *How to Meditate*, Thorsons (1995), 1 85538 277 6.

## Healing

Dossey, Larry, *Healing Words*, Harper Collins (1994), 0 06 250252 2.

## Massage

Macnamarra, Patricia, *Massage for People with Cancer*, Cancer Resource Centre, Wandsworth (1994), 0 95232243 9.

## Pain

Shone, Neville, *Coping Successfully with Pain*, Sheldon Press (1992), 0 85969 750 9.

## Death and Dying

Kubler-Ross, Elizabeth, *Wheel of Life*, Bantam (1998), 0 553 50544 0.

Levine, Stephen, *Healing into Life and Death*, Gateway Books (1987) 0 946551 48 0.

Levine, Stephen, *Meetings at the Edge*, Gateway Books (1984), 0 946551 88 X.

Nicholls, Ed, Elliot, Gill, and Elliott, Joseph, *New Natural Death Handbook*, Rider Books (1997), 0 7126 7111 0.

Rimpoche, Sogyal, *Tibetan Book of Living and Dying*, Rider Books (1992), 0 7126 7139 0.

## *Alternative Cancer Medicines*

Diamond, W John, Cowden, W Lee, and Goldberg, Burton, *Definitive Guide to Cancer*, Future Medicine Publishing Inc., 88729901 7.

## *Visualization*

Auchterberg, Jeanne, *Imagery in Healing*, Shamballa, (1985), 0 394 73031 3.

Gawler, Ian, *Creative Power of Imagery*, Hill of Content (1997), 0 85572 281 9.

Simonton, Carl, *Getting Well Again*, Bantam (1988), 0 553 28033 3.

Gawain, Shakti, *Creative Vizualization*, Bantam (1978), 0 553 27044 3.

# Audio Cassettes and CDs

## *Meditation*
Adams, Jenni, *Inner Silence.*
*Meditation Made Easy.*

## *Relaxation*
Adams, Jenni, *Relax and Sleep Well.*
Burling, Joy, *Relax with Joy.*

## *Yoga*
Siddall, Barbara, *Altered States 1.*
Morgan Tessa, *Yoga at Home.*

# *Index*

# Index